TWAYNE'S WORLD AUTHORS SERIES

A Survey of the World's Literature

Sylvia E. Bowman, Indiana University

GENERAL EDITOR

CHINA

William Schultz, University of Arizona

EDITOR

Kung Tzu–chen

TWAS 370

A page from a photolithographic reprint of Kung Tzu-chen's calligraphy showing the text of two of the Chi-hai quatrains.

KUNG TZU-CHEN

By SHIRLEEN S. WONG

University of California at Los Angeles

TWAYNE PUBLISHERS

A DIVISION OF G. K. HALL & CO., BOSTON

Library of Congress Cataloging in Publication Data

Wong, Shirleen S
Kung Tzu-chen.

(Twayne's world authors series; TWAS 370: China)
Bibliography: p. 171–75.
Includes index.
1. Kung, Tzu-chen, 1792-1841.
PL2717.U5Z88 1976   821'.8   75-15897
ISBN 0-8057-6184-5

To Professor Hsiao Kung-ch'üan
—poet, scholar, teacher—
for his 77th birthday

Contents

About the Author

Shirleen S. Wong was born in Macao (1940) and educated in Hong Kong and the United States, where she received a B.A. in history from Skidmore College in 1961, a M.A. in American history from Columbia University in 1963, and a Ph.D. in Chinese literature from the University of Washington in 1970. She taught European and American history at the Annie Wright Seminary at Tacoma, Washington, in 1963–64. Since 1968, she has been teaching Chinese language and literature at the University of California at Los Angeles. The author of an article on the T'ang poet Tu Fu, she is currently engaged in a study of the satiric voice in Ch'ing poetry.

Preface

Kung Tzu-chen, a forceful poetic voice from early nineteenth-century China, is one of those recalcitrant souls who defy labeling. He lived during a period when China was precariously poised between hoary tradition and impending change, and he wrote a wide range of poetry which often reveals a restless spirit beneath a cadenced classical language. Like most traditional Chinese men of letters reared in the Confucian ideal of public service and self-cultivation, he embodied the roles of both social critic and lyric poet. Yet, unlike most of his poetic peers, he showed an exceptional interest in recording the changing landscape of his own psyche, and wrote satiric verse imbued with great exuberance.

The historical Kung Tzu-chen was a multifaceted man of conflicting traits. As a historian, he foresaw the inevitable doom of the Ch'ing empire; yet he took the metropolitan examination six times in the hope of gaining a useful position in the official hierarchy. As a scholar versed in Buddhist philosophy, he placed little value in expressive language; yet he wrote eloquent prose and poetry of great diversity until the year he died. He was a "minor official" who advocated grand policies for saving a disintegrating imperial order, and a highly accomplished scholar who insisted on the insignificance of scholarship. In the end, history reconciled his contradictions for him. He was an extremely popular poet at the turn of this century, when the Ch'ing empire he tried to save was on the verge of total collapse, and a new breed of readers was looking for a native prophet.

In this study, I have approached Kung Tzu-chen mainly as an accomplished poet writing at a given juncture of a long and splendid tradition, not as a colorful historical personage. Biographical information is kept to a minimum in order to give more space to Kung's poetry. A total of ninety-six poems are translated and included in the course of discussion. Chapter One is a sketch of the poet's historical milieu, his various reactions to a disappointing public career, and his conception of language and poetry. Chapters Two and Three summarize the major themes and technical features of Kung's *shih* poetry as a whole, but exclude the 315 seven-character quatrains he wrote in the year Chi-hai (1839). Chapter Four treats the Chi-hai quatrains as exemplary pieces of the *chüeh-chü* genre, examining them against traditional Chinese critical and compositional criteria such as *han-hsü* (economy and suggestiveness) and *pien-hua* (variation and change). Chapter Five deals with Kung's *tz'u* lyrics from the perspective of the dream motif; the underlying assumption is that the poet's most personal moments are forged into the *tz'u*. Chapter Six takes the poet out of his private world of dreams and fantasies and places him in the stream of Chinese poetry; it also examines Kung's two favorite images—the flute and the sword—in their literary and historical contexts.

In order not to burden the nonspecialists—particularly those who do not have a reading knowledge of the Chinese language—with a bewildering amount of strange terms and digressive passages, I have provided a translation for every Chinese term used in the text and relegated most points of technical interest to the footnotes. Readers interested in pursuing further a given subject are urged to consult the footnote section.

I am aware that writing on a Ch'ing poet, especially a nineteenth-century transitional figure like Kung Tzu-chen, is a hazardous undertaking. There are many obstacles to overcome, the most difficult being the lack of historical perspective. Unlike the T'ang and Sung periods, whose contours have been revealed through repeated investigations, much of the history and development of Ch'ing poetry is still obscured by vague generalizations. The two ends of the Ch'ing period have received occasional attention; the mid-portion, the first half of the nineteenth century in particular, is largely an uncharted area. This study is a preliminary attempt to explore that neglected interval. Without the benefit of background information, however, what we glean from patient readings of one poet will likely be piecemeal revelations until further studies of this period yield enough patterns for us to assimilate into a historical context.

This book grew out of a doctoral dissertation which I wrote between 1968 and 1970. The book would not have been realized without the encouragement and help of several individuals. First of all, I would like to thank Professor Hellmut Wilhelm for his guidance during my student years at the University of Washington; I owe Professor Wilhelm a special debt of gratitude for serving as my dissertation chairman and for making the initial contact with the Twayne Publishers about revising the dissertation for publication. Professor Lao Kan, my mentor and senior colleague at U.C.L.A., answered many queries about textual matters concerning Kung Tzu-chen's writings, and his encyclopedic knowledge of Chinese literature and history saved me from taking many barren detours; I am most grateful to him for his patience and unfailing concern over the progress of the book. Professor Richard Rudolph, as chairman and acting chairman of the department, has made it possible for me to complete the manuscript without the distractions of practical concerns; I want to thank him sincerely for the generous and much-needed moral support he has given me over the past few years.

I am very grateful to my colleague Professor Robert Epp for reading the first three chapters of the preliminary draft and for volunteering his editorial help; he has been most generous with his time, an act of friendship which I greatly appreciate. Thanks are also due Mr. Philip Ardell for reading Chapters Four, Five, and Six. I owe my good friend, Hedy H. Lee, a heavy debt of gratitude for her insightful and often relentless criticisms regarding the overall approach of the study; her unerring sense of form and her insistence on larger perspectives have often sent me back to the same chapter several times. I owe her a profound apology for not having expanded the first three chapters as she suggested; there was a university administrative deadline to meet, and time simply did not allow.

Professor William Schultz, my editor, has been most patient and kind in every possible way; without his sustained interest in the subject and his timely encouragements, this book would have remained an unfinished project; I owe him a debt beyond words.

Professor Hsiao Kung-ch'üan, professor emeritus of the University of Washington, has read the entire manuscript with magnanimous tolerance and sent words of encouragement whenever they were needed. A man of great wit and wisdom, he seldom corrects without an understanding smile; and despite his own monumental achievements, he never turns away an inquiring student. With deep affection, I dedicate this book to him.

SHIRLEEN S. WONG

University of California at Los Angeles

Chronology

1792   Born in Hangchow, Chekiang, on the 5th day of the 7th lunar month (August 22). (*tzu*: Se-jen, *hao*: Ting-an; registered as a native of Jen-ho County, Chekiang)

1796   His father, Kung Li-cheng, obtains the *chin-shih* (metropolitan graduate) degree. (Rises to the position of Intendant of Soochow and Sungkiang, Kiangsu; retires in 1825.)

1798   His mother, Tuan Hsün, daughter of the famous philologist Tuan Yü-ts'ai, gives him his first lessons in poetry.

1802   Follows his father to Peking, the capital.

1803   Begins the study of etymology under the guidance of his maternal grandfather.

1810   Takes the provincial examination and succeeds in becoming an Imperial Student (*kung-sheng*) on a supplementary list (*fu-pang*). Begins to compose *tz'u* lyrics.

1812   Serves as collator in the Imperial Printing Office. In the 4th month, marries his cousin, Tuan Mei-chen, in Soochow; afterwards the couple returns to Hangchow.

1813   His wife dies.

1814   Writes four "Essays on the Enlightened [Ruler] and the Worthy [Minister]" (*Ming liang lun*).

1815   Marries his second wife, Ho Chi-yün.

1816   Finishes the series of essays entitled "Treatises of the Years I-hai and Ping-tzu" (*I-ping chih chi chu-i*).

1818   Passes the provincial examination in Chekiang and obtains the *chü-jen* (provincial graduate) degree.

1819   Fails the Metropolitan Examination by Virtue of Imperial Favor (*en-k'o hui-shih*). Studies the Kung-yang commentary to the *Spring and Autumn Annals* under Liu Feng-lu (1776—1829).

1820   Fails the metropolitan examination again. Serves as a secretary in the Grand Secretariat *(Nei-ko)*. Writes "Suggestions on Barring Foreign Ships from the Southeast" *(Tung-nan pa fan-po i)* and "Suggestions on Establishing a Province in the Western Territories" *(Hsi-yü chih hsing-sheng i)*. Autumn, vows to abstain from writing poetry.

1821   Serves as a redactor in the Grand Secretariat's Bureau of Dynastic History and participates in the revision of the *General Gazetteer of the Ch'ing Empire (Ta-ch'ing i-t'ung chih)*. Begins an extensive survey of Mongolia (finishes only several chapters of it). Summer, fails the examination for the Privy Council *(Chün-chi ch'u)*. Breaks his vow of abstention and writes a series of fifteen "Short Lyrics on Travels in the Immortals' Realm" *(Hsiao yu-hsien tz'u)*.

1823   Prints four collections of his *tz'u*. His mother dies.

1824   In mourning; does not compose any poems. Studies Buddhism.

1829   Finally passes the metropolitan examination (after five unsuccessful attempts) and obtains the rating of a third-rank *chin-shih* graduate at the palace examination. Appointed to the position of a magistrate but chooses to remain a secretary in the Grand Secretariat. Presents the "Letter to the Grand Secretary" *(Shang ta-hsüeh-shih shu)* to his superior, advocating various changes in the Grand Secretariat; his suggestions are not adopted.

1835   Transferred to the Imperial Clan Court *(Tsung-jen fu)*.

1837   Transferred to the Board of Rites *(Li-pu)*.

1838   Sends a letter to Imperial Commissioner Lin Tse-hsü before Lin departs from Peking for Canton to take charge of the campaign against opium; stresses that the outflow of silver from China and the importation of woolens must also be stopped. (Lin replies in general agreement with Kung, but declines the latter's offer of assistance.)

1839   Resigns from the Board of Rites and leaves the capital for Hangchow. Writes the "Miscellaneous Poems of the Year Chi-hai" *(Chi-hai tsa-shih)*.

1840   Compiles the "Elegant Lyrics of the Year Keng-tzu" *(Keng-tzu ya-tz'u)*.

1841   Sets out for Tan-yang, Kiangsu, to assume a teaching post during spring. On the 5th day of the 3rd lunar month, his father dies. On the 12th day of the 8th lunar month (September 26), the poet dies of a sudden illness at Tan-yang; leaves two sons: Ch'eng and T'ao, and two daughters: Hsin and A-ch'un. (Kung T'ao later becomes a magistrate.)

List of Translations

Tz'u Lyrics by Kung Tzu-chen:

Shih and *Tz'u* by Other Poets:

CHAPTER 1

Starter of Trends:
Life and Times of the Poet

Historians did not believe that Wang T'ung had
  prime ministers among his disciples.[1]
The commoner's prestige and status have always been low.
In my life one thing causes no back-biting:
I only start trends, never become a teacher.
    —*Miscellaneous Poems of the Year Chi-hai* (1839), No. 104

BORN in 1792, toward the end of the Ch'ien-lung era, Kung Tzu-chen lived during the turning point of the Ch'ing dynasty. The impact of such an age of transition on Kung's life, ideas, and literary expressions can hardly be exaggerated. While signs of decline were apparent everywhere to the discerning few, the majority of officials still indulged in a false sense of strength and affluence following over a century of internal peace and well-being under the reigns of the K'ang-hsi, Yung-cheng, and Ch'ien-lung Emperors. The first eye-opening blow to Chinese supremacy, the Opium War, did not break out until the year before Kung's death in 1841, and the ordeal of the T'ai-p'ing Rebellion (1850–64) was another decade away. As a result, Kung's many criticisms and comments on political and economic problems fell on deaf ears, his official career became a source of frustration, and he had no choice but to channel his unusual talents into scholarly and literary endeavors.

At the same time, the first half of the nineteenth century saw the relaxation of the literary inquisition instituted by the Manchu rulers who formerly had silenced many perceptive individuals, like the

21

"ten thousand muted horses" Kung observed in one of his poems.[2] This made it possible for Kung to turn away from the politically harmless pursuit of textual criticism, which preoccupied the scholars of the Ch'ien-lung and the Chia-ch'ing periods, and insist that scholarship should be put to the service of practical issues.[3] In his commitment to this end, Kung has significantly influenced later reformers. As attested to by Liang Ch'i-ch'ao, a leader of the Hundred Days Reforms in 1898, "Kung Tzu-chen has undoubtedly contributed to the emancipation of thought in late Ch'ing times. Practically all of the so-called new scholars during the reign of Kuang-hsü have admired Kung at one time or another. On first reading his collected essays, one is electrified."[4] Thus, true to the statement made in the poem above, Kung initiated a trend in the intellectual and literary history of the Ch'ing dynasty by giving new impetus to and a new perspective on the book learning of his age.

I *The Times*

Many factors in the decline of the Ch'ing dynasty can be traced to the latter part of the long reign of the Ch'ien-lung Emperor (1736–95).[5] Among these factors was official corruption as exemplified by the case of the Manchu chief minister Ho-shen. When Ho-shen was removed from office and executed by the Chia-ch'ing Emperor in 1799, after twenty years in power, the property he had accumulated was estimated at eight hundred million *taels*. With the government's annual income then being around seventy million, this is approximately equivalent to governmental revenues for a period of eleven years, or, to put it differently, more than half of the government's annual income went into Ho-shen's pocket.[6] Nor were the officials of native Chinese origin less corrupt. According to Chang Hsüeh-ch'eng (1738–1801), a fellow countryman of Kung's from Chekiang province, in the officialdom of that time "superiors and subordinates deceive one another for the sole purpose of corruption and bribery. At first they gnaw away like a silkworm, then they gradually swallow everything like a whale. In the beginning, hundreds and thousands are involved. Soon, anything less than ten thousand has to be multiplied several times. Finally, it becomes hundreds of thousands and several millions."[7]

On the heels of increasing corruption among government officials came a fall in the market value of copper coins and a rise in the price of silver. The farmers suffered, in particular, because taxes were paid in silver and farm products were sold only for copper. Although many factors affected the copper-silver exchange rate, Chinese authorities blamed the problem on the opium trade, which drained away the supply of silver in China; thus officials neglected making the proper and necessary currency reforms.[8] In the meantime, prices in general climbed. Perhaps one of the best ways to document these phenomena is to quote two of Kung's poems: the first satirizes rising food prices; the second laments the cumbersome tax schemes in the southeastern provinces, while other sources of revenue, like the government monopolies of salt and iron and the administration of the Yellow River, were neglected.

Cookie Song

> Elders with one green coin,[9]
> A cookie round as the moon.
> Children with two green coins,
> A cookie big as a coin.
> The cookie on the plate costs one more coin,
> The moon in the sky shrinks on one edge.
> Alas! food in the market. Oh! moon in the sky.
> I can predict, oh, the wax and wane of you two.
> You two which are like passers-by.
> Moon speaks to cookie:
> > The round one should wane.
> Cookie speaks to moon:
> > The cycle is endless.
> That which is big as a coin,
> Should again be round as the moon.
> Come children, let me tell you:
> > Five hundred years hence,
> > Your grandsons' grandsons will be full.   [K 462–63]

Miscellaneous Poems of the Year Chi-hai   [No. 123]

> Without discussing salt and iron, without
> > draining the River,
> The burden falls on the southeast alone,
> > the cause of many tears.
> Three pints of state tax cost the people a peck,
> Won't butchering the ox be better than raising crops![10]   [K 521]

In addition to bureaucratic and economic problems, China in Kung's time was also faced with a population explosion. The reasons often given to account for this are the long duration of internal peace; the introduction and widespread use of European food crops, such as maize and sweet potatoes; and the subsequent cultivation of new land on the hillsides. This last practice turned out to be shortsighted, for the resultant deforestation and soil erosion caused far greater damage than the new tillage was worth. But, confronted with the increasing size of his family and the limited amount of tillable land, the Chinese farmer had little choice. Although statistics vary as to the number and extent of this increase in population,[11] here is a description of its impact by an eyewitness, Hung Liang-chi (1746–1809):

I have heard that fifty years ago, at the time of my grandfather and my father, each pint of rice cost only six or seven coins, and every ten feet of cloth only thirty or forty. . . . Now it is different. The number of farmers is ten times greater than before but the tillage has not increased. The number of merchants is ten times greater than before but the goods have not increased. The number of scholars is ten times greater than before but schools for them to teach at have not increased. Moreover, each pint of rice costs thirty or forty coins, and every ten feet of cloth costs one or two hundred. The smaller the income, the greater the expenditure. . . . Besides, since the population is ten times greater than before, the number of wandering vagabonds multiplies even more. In the event of flood, drought, or epidemic, it is obvious that they would not just sit back and wait for death.[12]

The accuracy of Hung's observation was borne out by popular uprisings, beginning with the first major one in Shantung in 1774.[13] The next year, another movement gathered momentum in Honan, led by members of a secret organization known as the White Lotus Society. Before this group was finally suppressed in 1802, it had infested several provinces, entailed the expenditure of two hundred million *taels* of state revenue,[14] and brought about repressive measures by the government, the severity of which is shown by the beheading of over 20,000 people within four months in the city of Wu-ch'ang.[15] In 1813, the Society of Heaven's Law, another secret organization, rose near Peking and even made an attempt on the life of the Chia-ch'ing Emperor. In 1832, aboriginal tribesmen in Kiangsi and Hunan also rebelled.[16] Although these revolts were quelled by the government, they reflected the impoverishment of the masses and paved the way for greater disorders.

In the light of these signs of trouble, it is not surprising that late in 1840, after the outbreak of the Opium War and the removal of Commissioner Lin Tse-hsü from office, Kung Tzu-chen had the following to say in a letter to a friend:

In recent years, you may want to stop the people from smoking opium, but the people would not let you. This is an age in which slaves usurp the places of their masters and grandsons beat up their grandfathers. Even if England did not encroach upon us or rebel [*sic*] against us, and respectfully rendered monetary tribute to us instead, China would still be in a shameful and lamentable state. I wish those in charge of affairs would not be so concerned with England! [K 341]

II *Words of a Minor Official*

Born in a family which had already served the government for two generations, Kung lived in Peking between the ages of eleven and twenty-one.[17] He thus acquired a firsthand knowledge of official life. The policy of direct imperial rule, adopted by the Ch'ing emperors to bypass the official hierarchy, at first successfully re-duced bureaucratic red tape and abuses.[18] By this time, however, direct rule had degenerated into mere autocratic arrogance, ac-companied by excessive rules of etiquette in observance of which a minister had to behave like a servant, stripped of all sense of dignity or shame.[19] Therefore, as early as 1814, at the tender age of twenty-three, Kung wrote a series of four "Essays on the En-lightened [Ruler] and the Worthy [Minister]" (*Ming liang lun*) to assail the shameless subjugation of the scholar-officials. "If all scholars have a sense of shame, then the country will never suffer from shame. Scholars with no sense of shame are the great shame of the country," begins one essay.[20] On this basis, Kung called for the restoration of the ruler's respect for his ministers, as was true of past dynasties, and the return of a reasonable amount of autonomy. "All are ancient prescriptions," commented Kung's maternal grand-father, the famous philologist Tuan Yü-ts'ai, "but they hit right at today's illnesses."[21]

Two years later, Kung completed the series of essays entitled "Treatises of the Years I-hai and Ping-tzu [1815–16]" (*I-Ping chih chi chu-i*) which attacks the separation of scholarship and government, warns of signs of decadence in spite of the appearance of prosperity, and, above all, in the seventh essay clearly expounds the sig-nificance of reform:

There are no regulations of one ancestor which do not become outdated. There are no opinions of the multitude which do not prevail. Rather than leaving reform to posterity, it is better to carry out the reform oneself. Furthermore, consider why our ancestors flourished: was it not because of their reforming the decadence of the previous age? And consider the reason why the previous age flourished: was it not because of its reforming the decadence of the age before it? Why have there been so many changes and not one House ruling forever? Why has Heaven never been pleased with just one House? Why have the spirits never received offerings from just one House? Take heed! Take heed! [K 6]

Of the institutions needing reform, the one that affected scholars most was the system of civil service examinations. Kung himself suffered considerably under it. He had failed the metropolitan examination in Peking (hui-shih) five times before he finally passed it in 1829 at the age of thirty-eight.[22] Still, when he tried for the decisive palace examination (tien-shih) a month and a half later, he only obtained the rating of a third-rank chin-shih graduate because his handwriting was not considered to be in the proper style. Consequently he was not appointed to the esteemed Han-lin Academy.[23] Rather than accepting the appointment as a magistrate, Kung chose to remain in his post as a secretary, first in the Grand Secretariat or Cabinet (Nei-ko), then in the Imperial Clan Court (Tsung-jen fu), and finally on the Board of Rites (Li-pu). Small wonder that the examination system became a focal point of his satire and call for reforms. Writing in his "Self-Preface to the New Studies on Office Seeking" (Kan-lu hsin-shu tzu-hsü) a few years later, Kung sarcastically observed that although the Han-lin Academy produced many prime ministers and ranking officials in the Ch'ing dynasty, the qualification for its admission was only a matter of handwriting. Thus scholars like himself had better be trained in the various aspects of calligraphy, including five different ways of grinding ink sticks.[24] Nonetheless, the very fact that Kung had made so many attempts at the examinations reveals how much passing them must have meant to him; perhaps not merely for the sake of an office, but for the opportunity to realize some of his political ideals. Needless to say, such a vital concern inevitably found expression in his poetry, as will be seen in the next chapter.

Two other areas of deep concern often mentioned in Kung's poems are the frontier district of the northwest and the coastal region of the southeast. According to his note to one of the Mis-

cellaneous Poems of the Year Chi-hai (*Chi-hai tsa-shih*), Kung had written two essays in 1820, entitled "Suggestions on Establishing a Province in the Western Territories" (*Hsi-yü chih hsing-sheng i*) and "Suggestions on Barring Foreign Ships from the Southeast" (*Tung-nan pa fan-po i*). In the former, he advocates the utilization of the resources of the northwest to alleviate population pressures and the general impoverishment of the country. In his opinion, the government should encourage and subsidize the colonization of Turkestan by the unemployed and lawless members of the populace, especially those in Peking and nearby provinces like Shantung, Honan, Shensi, and Kansu.[25] Extensive plans were laid out by Kung for this purpose, but he was not to see their realization in his lifetime. Writing in 1839, in confident recollection of these suggestions, Kung laments:

> Within fifty years these words are bound
>   to come true,
> Words of this minor official in the vast
>   universe. [K 516]

His prediction came true in 1884, when Turkestan was made into a province after its reconquest by Tso Tsung-t'ang.[26] Therefore, Kung later received a posthumous acclamation by no less an authority than the statesman and diplomat Li Hung-chang (1823–1901). In his "Preface to a Brief Account of the Black Dragon River" (*Hei-lung-chiang shu-lüeh hsü*), Li remarks:

The initiation of extraordinary projects often comes from the anxious and worried thoughts of scholars. Kung Tzu-chen suggested the establishment of a province in the Western Territories in the reign of Tao-kuang[27] and it is finally being carried out on a large scale today.[28]

As for the southeast, the reasons for Kung's interest are obvious. Besides being his native country, the provinces of Kiangsu and Chekiang also constituted one nucleus of China's wealth and learning. According to the census of the Ch'ien-lung era, the population of the single prefecture of Yangchow already exceeded that of the whole province of Chihli, and the population of the prefecture of Sung-chiang surpassed that of the provinces of Honan, Shansi, Shensi, and Kansu respectively. Yangchow was also a chief center of salt manufacture, with sufficient funds to encourage

cultural developments in both Kiangsu and Chekiang.[29] The leading
position of this region in arts and letters can be gathered from the
fact that of the seven copies of the nearly seventeen thousand
volumes collected in the Ch'ien-lung Emperor's epoch-making
"Complete Collection of Books on the Four Branches of Learning"
(Ssu-k'u ch'üan-shu), the three which were not kept in the palace
libraries were deposited there.[30] A look at the statistics of successful
candidates in the metropolitan examinations in Peking also shows
that Kiangsu and Chekiang excelled the other provinces.[31]

Although Kung's essay on barring foreign ships from the southeast
is no longer extant,[32] his concern over foreign infringement can be
seen in a letter sent to Commissioner Lin Tse-hsü before the latter
departed from Peking for Canton to take charge of the campaign
against opium. In it, Kung stressed that the outflow of silver from
China must be stopped, opium smokers and dealers should be
deterred by capital punishment, and that not only opium but the
importation of woolens also ought to be barred in order to protect
domestic industries.[33] Lin's reply agreed with Kung's views in
general but expressed caution with regard to possible opposition
from the court. Within two years, a battle with British ships erupted
in Canton and Lin was accused of mishandling the situation, removed from office, and later exiled to far away Ili.[34] Kung himself
died before the settlement of the Opium War.

III   Reforms but not Revolution

Having so keenly discerned the various signs of decline around
him, Kung Tzu-chen foresaw at a very early stage the imminence of
disaster. In the ninth essay of the 1815–16 series mentioned above,
Kung says prophetically that "When I rise to look at the age, disor-
der is not far away."[35] In the "Discourse on Equalization" (P'ing-
chün p'ien) written at about the same time,[36] Kung again hints at
impending doom in the observation "Animals and humans alike are
in grief and pain while the spirits and deities are contemplating a
change of position,"[37] the last expression (pien chih) being taken
from a passage in the Mencius which refers to a change of political
power. Even more prophetic and much more obscure is the extraordinary essay "Revering the Recluse" (Tsun yin), also written
early in the author's life.[38] Here, under the cloak of supernatural
images, fanciful personifications, and archaic terminology, Kung
launches a sweeping attack on the Ch'ing dynasty. In spite of its

ancient setting and the archaic effect of numerous repetitions, the whole essay bursts with the vitality of youth. Poignant remarks roll from one line into the next. Different ideas are often strung into flowing sentences held together by the sheer force of the prose. Yet, disguises and embellishments notwithstanding, the central prophecy is unmistakable. After the description of the steady decline of the capital and the consolidation of the "inhabitants of the mountains," there is the following turn of events:

Suddenly, all is silent. The lamps and candles die out. No more words are heard; there is only the sound of snoring. In the long, long night, no *ho-tan* bird [which heralds the coming of dawn] sings. Then, a great cry breaks out among the inhabitants of the mountains. Heaven and earth resound like bells and drums, and the gods are swayed by it.   [K 88]

Incredible though it may seem, considering that Kung wrote this at least thirty years before the T'ai-p'ing Rebellion, its implication is clear: before the break of dawn upon the darkness of the present age, there will be a major upheaval, or perhaps even a revolution.

However, in order to understand Kung's attitude and especially the poems he wrote later in life, it must be pointed out that vehement though his criticisms and predictions undoubtedly were, Kung never abandoned his loyalty to the Ch'ing dynasty. Even after he had resigned his office in the capital, he still clung, with great relish, to the memories of his career as a minor official, as in the following poem. The Ch'ien-ch'ing Gate refers to the entrance to the palace where the emperor held court, outside of which the heavy morning dew soaked the officials' robes:

Miscellaneous Poems of the Year Chi-hai   [No. 6]

I have also served at the Grand Secretariat[39] with
    my books and brushes.
In a heavenly midnight breeze the jade
    bridle-bells kept me company.[40]
I want to launder my spring robe, but refrain
    out of tender regard
For the traces of dewdrops from outside
    the Ch'ien-ch'ing Gate.   [K 509]

From such fond nostalgia for the court expressed in this and other poems, particularly those with the personal symbol of fallen flowers which will be discussed in Chapter Four, we may venture to say that perhaps Kung criticised the dynasty so unrelentingly because of his attachment to it and therefore was trying to ward off the catastrophe he foresaw. The important "Letter to the Grand Secretary" (*Shang ta-hsüeh-shih shu*), presented to his superior in 1829 and advocating various changes in the Grand Secretariat, confirms this view. Kung explained at the outset:

From antiquity to the present, there were no laws which remained unaltered, no conditions which did not result from accumulated [evils], no customs which did not change, no trends which did not shift. The only basis one can rely on is the inexhaustible supply of talent in the world. . . . Those who feel strongly about things and occupy high positions have the authority to carry out what they consider to be right and remove what they consider to be wrong. Those who feel strongly about things but occupy only low positions do not have the authority. Then they can examine what they consider right or wrong and speak out loudly about it. This way, where is the harm of altering laws? Where is the weight of accumulated conditions? Where is the danger of shifting trends? Where is the fear of changing customs? [K 319]

That Kung was more concerned than resentful toward the dynasty can also be seen in the conclusion of a letter to a friend written the year before he died: "My state of mind is rather calm these days. Although I am far away among the rivers and lakes, I bear no grudges, thinking very much of the capital and the nation."[41] Thus, unlike the interpretation of some overly eager scholars,[42] what Kung really wanted was reform, not revolution.

IV *From Madness to Trivialities*

Well-meaning though he was, a message such as that in "Revering the Recluse" would have meant certain persecution if not carefully concealed under the guise of antiquity and the obscurity of the language. This is one reason why so many of Kung's prose pieces are written in a deliberately strange style. For example, in the three essays on "Catches" (*pu*), in which Kung discourses on the ancient methods of catching different kinds of animals and insects,[43] the contents are so out of the ordinary that a censor would not likely have found anything political in them. Yet no one who takes Kung seriously would think that these are merely exercises in fantasy. These essays could easily have been ways of satirizing the various vices of the time; after all, species like the toad, the owl, and the

wolf are no strangers in the long tradition of Chinese political alle-
gory. At any rate, partly due to such careful concealment and partly
due to the relaxation of censorship during the Chia-ch'ing and Tao-
kuang reigns, Kung Tzu-chen was never censured by the government in spite of the provocative potential of his writings.

There was, however, another consequence of this concealment.
Given the unappreciative blindness of his age and the insignificance
of his official position as a secretary, Kung's angry outcries seemed
all the more bizarre to his contemporaries and contributed to his
reputation as a man of mad abandonment (*k'uang*). Judging from the
various accounts of his dashing personality, Kung himself might
have purposely cultivated this image. For what better way was there
to express his frustrated ambitions and talents?

As a result, the picture Kung leaves behind as a private person is
clouded with exaggeration and hearsay. He was supposed to be a
spendthrift and a gambler. According to one account, he had
numbers drawn on the canopy above his bed so that during his free
moments he could stretch out and unravel the mathematics involved in gambling, since he usually lost.[44] Other anecdotes foster-
ing the image of mad abandonment abound. One story appears in
"Anecdotes of the Mountain Dweller at Yü-ling" (*Yü-ling shan-min
i-shih*), written by a grandson of Wei Yüan (1794–1856), who was
one of Kung's close friends and fellow scholars. One evening when
Kung was visiting the Wei household, so the tale goes, he became so
absorbed in talking with some friends in the garden that when he
finally got up to see the friends off, he could not find his boots. The
boots were found several days later on top of the awning under
which they talked. Apparently Kung, who had perched on a table,
grew so animated during the discussion, and so flailed his arms and
legs about, that he had unknowingly kicked off his boots.[45]

The same source also tells several interesting stories about Kung's
appearance. He was short, homely, and apparently unconcerned
about his looks. One day he called on Wei Yüan in a coat of white fox
fur, the bottom half of which was caked with mud. When asked
about it, Kung said it was snowing heavily on his way to the Wei's
and a friend took off his own fur coat for Kung to wear. As the friend
was considerably taller, Kung had simply let the fur coat drag on the
ground.[46]

Many anecdotes of Kung which have appeared in modern
newspaper or magazine articles are obviously unreliable, often just
recalled from memory with the original reference already forgotten.

Rather than furthering the eccentric picture of Kung presented by these apparently biased fictions, it is preferable to look into a more serious attempt at collecting the scattered information on Kung, namely, Chang Tsu-lien's *Records in Addition to the Chronological Biography of Mr. Ting-an* (*Ting-an hsien-sheng nien-p'u wai-chi*); Ting-an is the sobriquet, or *hao*, of Kung.

In this series of fragmentary records, we are reminded of the fact that besides the eccentric nicknamed by some acquaintances as "Kung the Bookish Fool" (*Kung tai-tzu*), there is also Kung the poet. Early in his childhood, Kung aroused the admiration of neighbors by playing a flute one spring night on a storeyed building above the lake, to the tune of "Song of the Cave Elves" (*Tung-hsien ko*) by the Sung poet Su Shih (1037–1101).[47] It was this aspect of his personality which manifested itself when Kung rode alone through the capital on a donkey-cart to where peonies were in full bloom, then sat on the ground drinking and singing with a passerby until the petals came floating down around him.[48] This was the Kung who could compose brilliant poetry or prose on the spur of the moment,[49] who was a connoisseur and avid collector of ancient inscriptions, a specialist in Manchurian and Mongolian linguistics, and a zealous traveler whose sojourns covered many parts of the Chinese empire and enriched much of his prose and poetry.[50] As Kung indicates in the following poem that deals with his writings in archaeology and epigraphy, all these diverse interests, which he refers to as trivialities (*so*), served as outlets for his political craving and unusual talents; the latter he refers to as "strange forces" (*ch'i ch'i*):

Miscellaneous Poems of the Year Chi-hai [No. 73]

> Once released, strange forces cannot be confined.
> Indulging in trivialities—a tactic to erode the strange.
> But the strange is eroded while the trivialities remain,
> Arrayed before my eyes like the Five Mountains.[51]   [K 516]

V *Condoning Emotion and Escaping to Zen*

When even trivialities proved to be inadequate and boring, Kung turned to romantic adventures and Buddhism. As a contemporary said of him after he had resigned his office in the capital, he was either seeking entertainment in the gay quarters or visiting Buddhist monks.[52] Kung himself elucidated the situation in a *tz'u* lyric: "Persons of talent in their declining years escape to Zen."[53] The element of intentional escape from the frustration of his official career and a futile existence in retirement is also explicit in many of his poems about women. For example:

> Having dissipated talents which could sway the nation,
> I am content to serve a woman, to wait upon her
>   liquid glances. [K 532]
>
>   . . . .
>
> But today I no longer shed my idle tears;
> In crossing the river, I miss only her charming
>   presence. [K 519]
>
>   . . . .
>
> Imagine a hero in his declining years:
> Where can he dwell but in the land of love?[54] [534]

Some high-minded critics, however, do not seem to take this element into consideration when they denounce Kung's personal life. The many-sided scholar Wang Kuo-wei (1877–1927), for instance, singles out one of Kung's love poems as the basis for his condemnation: "Kung's heartless superficiality and irresponsible conduct pop right out of his lines. There is no need to study his life history to know his corruptness!"[55]

In the light of what has been said thus far, such a judgment is too harsh. After all, even Wang himself had occasion to acquiesce in abandonment:

> Let me just be dead drunk by a farm house,
> And for the time being rest from my journey
>   at the hermit's divination shop;[56]
> In this world of dust, one should only play.[57]

Kung, on his part, wrote an essay entitled "Condoning Emotion" (*Yu ch'ing*), anticipating future judgment.[58]

VI *Sudden Death and Speculations*

Moral principles aside, Kung's sudden death made his romantic adventures the object of much argument among scholars. In 1839, Kung resigned his position with the Board of Rites and returned to his native city of Hangchow, leaving his family in Peking. Later that year, he went up north again to bring his family back but did not enter the capital himself. In the spring of 1841, he started teaching at Tan-yang in the province of Kiangsu; a few months later he suddenly died.

Predictably, many have suggested the possibility of intrigue or poisoning rather than natural causes as the reason for Kung's sudden demise. Some think a favorite lady friend by the name of Ling-hsiao poisoned him because she had found a new love.[59] Others think a Yangchow prostitute called Hsiao-yün poisoned him, though no one is certain of her motive.[60] These speculations apparently derive from the fact that Kung mentioned these women in several of his poems.[61] This source of evidence also suggests a third possible cause of his death, namely, that the Imperial Clansman I-hui, a great-grandson of the Ch'ien-lung Emperor, poisoned Kung because of an affair with I-hui's concubine, the famous poetess Ku-t'ai-ch'ing.[62] Since the various arguments regarding this proposition are related to Kung's poetry, they warrant more detailed discussion.

One of the persons responsible for the spread of this third speculation was Mao Kuang-sheng (1876–?). When Mao printed the collected works of Ku-t'ai-ch'ing (the *T'ien-yu-ko chi*) in 1908, he added six quatrains of his own which are supposed to reflect the life history of the poetess. One reads:

> T'ai-p'ing Lane runs along T'ai-p'ing Lake;
> They buried Yeh-lai[63] in Southern Valley at the height
>   of spring;
> She could crush a city, her name crush a state.
> Whenever lilacs bloom, one lingers with fond memories.[64]

The first line gives the location of her residence; the second indicates where she was buried. The third line describes her beauty and hints at her surname, Ku; it is based on the well-known line of Li Yen-nien (2nd cent. B.C.): "One look [*ku*] could crush a city, another look [*ku*] could crush a state." The fourth line refers to the burgeoning rumor of the so-called "Lilac Case" (*Ting-hsiang-hua kung-an*) which links Ku with Kung Tzu-chen. For, in No. 209 of his Chi-hai poems, Kung wrote:

> Lingering on a desolate mountain, tired with travel,
> I dream of spring in the ethereal park west of the city,
> Where, as dusk descended on the vermilion mansion,
>   a horseman once delivered a letter
> To the one dressed in white,[65] facing the breeze.   [K 529]

Then he specified in the footnote to this poem, "In remembrance of the lilacs at Lake T'ai-p'ing inside the Hsüan-wu Gate." Thus, the object of Kung's affection became identified with Ku-t'ai-ch'ing, who did live by that lake. This association was even fictionalized in a chapter of the popular novel *Nieh-hai hua*. [66]

Familiar names are also featured on the other side of the argument. Meng Sen wrote an article entitled "Lilacs" in his book *Hsin-shih ts'ung-k'an* to refute Mao. Meng's main contention is that there are chronological discrepancies, not only in Kung's *shih* and *tz'u* pertinent to the case, but also in the ages of the three people involved. In the year Chi-hai, Kung was forty-eight, Ku was forty-one, and I-hui had been dead for a year. In Meng's opinion, both Kung and Ku were then too old for the alleged improper conduct, and a dead Imperial Clansman would not likely be an instigator of revenge. Moreover, judging from the many farewell poems Kung had written to his colleagues, he did not seem to have left the capital in a great hurry. The fact that he did not enter it again when he came back for his family might simply be due to his mood at that moment. As for the so-called "lilac poem," the vermilion mansion could indeed be Ku's residence and the "one dressed in white" Kung's wife. Ku was known to have befriended many of the womenfolk of officials in the capital. Meng therefore finds nothing unusual in her giving some lilacs to Kung's wife. Kung later commemorated the incident probably because these lilacs, not native to the area, were rare in Peking. [67]

Ch'ien Mu in his *Chung-kuo chin san-pai-nien hsüeh-shu shih* also doubts the credibility of the Ku–Kung rumor. His reasoning is that if Kung really had to leave the capital because of such an affair, he would have been more secretive about it instead of versifying upon it so much. Ch'ien accordingly offers yet another explanation, told to him by Chang Erh-t'ien (1884–?), which ascribes Kung's leaving Peking to his belligerent stand on the opium issue and the consequent antagonism between Kung and the Manchurian Chief Grand Councilor Mu-chang-a. [68]

Further suggestions are made by Wang Shou-nan, who has written one of the chronological biographies of Kung. Wang cites four possibilities as to why Kung had to leave the capital in 1839: (1) he had possibly offended one of his superiors; (2) he may have resigned out of frustration at remaining a minor official in the capital for over ten years; (3) Kung's father was then over seventy years old and this might constitute another reason why Kung wanted to return to his native place; and (4) furthermore, one of Kung's uncles had just become a ranking official on the Board of Rites where Kung served as a secretary. Under such circumstances, it was customary for a relative to dissociate himself from the Board. With the likelihood of personal revenge discarded, Wang concludes that Kung must have died of natural causes, such as a stroke or a heart attack.[69] This conclusion is strengthened by the fact that in 1837 Kung wrote in a letter to a friend that he had vomited half a pint of blood "due to homesickness and pent-up grievances."[70]

The most extensive discussion of the matter, thirty pages in all, is given by Su Hsüeh-lin. Her article is also most relevant to the interest of this book since it draws heavily on the evidence in Kung's poems. After examining some of the favorite terms used in his love lyrics, especially the collection entitled *Wu-cho tz'u*, or *Unfettered Lyrics*, Su proposes three hypotheses. First, Kung might really have had a secret connection with a Manchu lady of noble family, though she was definitely not Ku-t'ai-ch'ing. Second, this *tz'u* collection might be about an imaginary love affair invented by Kung out of playfulness or perversion. Or, and this is an intriguing possibility, the noble lady might be a symbol, not just of an ideal or a virtue as is common in Chinese poetic tradition, but of Kung's inner self, the source of his literary inspiration.[71] Here Su has indeed chanced upon an important revelation. Personal symbols of literary inspiration permeate Kung's poems, as will be seen in the next chapter.

VII   *Attitude Toward Literature and Poetry*

From all that has been said above, we may conclude that Kung's lifelong objective was active political service. All his romantic adventures and his excursions into various fields of scholarship and literature were only calculated distractions from a frustrated official career. When he was only twenty-two, his maternal grandfather, Tuan Yü-ts'ai, who had been greatly amazed by his literary talent, admonished him in a letter saying: "Do not study worthless books. Do not compose useless writings . . . Apply yourself to become a renowned scholar (*ming-ju*) and a renowned minister (*ming-ch'en*). Don't ever aspire to become a literary dilettante (*ming-shih*)."[72] As for his own attitude toward literary endeavors, Kung wrote in two of his *tz'u* poems: "Petty merits, ornate writings,/How could they be the aim of my life!"[73] "Even though my writings may startle the empire,/They contain nothing but living beings on paper."[74]

As far as his poetry was concerned, Kung thought the poems he wrote in his youth were among his best.[75] Unfortunately, most of these are no longer extant. Besides the possibility that some of Kung's unpublished manuscripts might have been scattered or destroyed during the T'ai-p'ing Rebellion,[76] it has been suggested that perhaps he burned some of his early works himself.[77] This is not so far-fetched when we consider the vows Kung made to abstain from writing poetry (*chieh-shih*), an undertaking hardly common among poets. There were at least three such attempts: one at the age of twenty-nine, another at thirty-six, and yet another at forty-seven. Needless to say, he broke his vow every time. Between the first and the second abstentions, he wrote 290 poems, 128 of which were grouped into the collection entitled *Abstinence-Breaking Scribbles (P'o-chieh ts'ao)*. The third abstention was followed by the 315 Chi-hai poems which represent the last upsurge of creativity in his life.[78]

The reason for Kung's efforts to abstain from writing poetry will be discussed in the next chapter, together with the main themes of his poems. That he failed in his attempts every time is an illustration of his compulsion to write at the urge of emotions or circumstances, be it the social and political conditions of his time, the frustration of his official career, or the dictates of his heart. "I have not written a single letter discussing literature," Kung wrote to a friend.[79] This is another indication of the fact that Kung's writings are all responses to actual experiences and feelings rather than to abstract principles, as will be seen in the following pages.

CHAPTER 2

The Flute and the Sword:
Favorite Symbols, Images, and Themes

Gone is my plan of being a soldier on the far frontier.
Quiet grievances fill my poems in this southeastern area.
The flute and the sword, the two goals of my life,
Have made me endure the name of madman for fifteen years.
—"Stray Thoughts" [K 467]

KUNG'S poetry, like his prose, is known for its unusual expressions and obscurity. Some of his lines read like riddles. Nevertheless, certain terms and subjects recur frequently enough in his comprehensible poems to suggest a consistency in meaning and usage which calls for an attempt at interpretation. The purpose of this chapter is to clarify the metaphorical implications of some of his favorite symbols and images, and to demonstrate the interrelatedness of his major themes.

I The Flute and the Sword

Just as the southeast and the northwest constitute focal areas in Kung's essays, the flute and the sword recur in his poems as symbols of poetic expression and heroic deeds, reflecting his dual emphasis on aesthetics and action. This is true of the poem quoted above, in which the flute is clearly associated with poetry and the sword with defense. They are also identified both as the poet's lifelong objectives and as the leaven of his unbridled emotions. Similar symbolic associations and geographical counterparts appear in the following poem which begins with a lament for his beloved who is beyond recall, but whose personal possessions still remain to evoke tender

memories. His longing and isolation remind the poet of the lack of
forceful warriors on the northwestern frontier and the scarcity of
poets in the southeast, his native country. The concluding lines may
indicate his solitary and unappreciated state, where he sees himself
as a lone moon among countless stars.

Autumn Thoughts [No. 1]

Autumn thoughts swell like the sea and its tide,
But the soul of autumn can no longer be summoned.
Faint, faint, the fragrance of herb ointment lingers
    on my arms;
Bright, bright, the ornament of ancient jade glows
    at my waist.
Whose icy sword guards the northwest?
How many flute songs fill the southeast?
Countless huge stars glisten
As the moon sinks across the long sky into the tree tops.
                                        [K 479]

Another example of the pairing of the flute and the sword occurs
in a poem that deplores the tumultuous nature of creativity. This
turmoil has survived even the fire of world destruction at the end of
a *kalpa,* the Buddhist concept of a cosmic cycle. On the concrete
side, such creative energy expresses itself in the writng of practical
treatises and, at its height, must be vented by vigorous action such
as the brandishing of a sword. On the abstract side, this creative
energy takes the form of spellbinding insights and intuitions which,
as they attenuate, leave a residue of sentiment more in consonance
with music and poetry than with a sword. The terms "wild intuitions" and "mental cure," referring to unchanneled thoughts and
the healing effect of religion, are also of Buddhist origin.

Repenting My Mind's Turmoil

Buddha said the fire of *kalpa* consumes everything in its
    path:
What has been raging for a thousand years like tidal
    waves?
Essays on state matters wear away my days;
Subtle insights and wild intuitions possess my nights.
They come in angry torrents and I must brandish my sword;

They leave a lingering flavor appropriate to the flute.
Mental cure and mental brilliance both indicate a
    troubled mind;
I am determined to set fire to my allegories.[1]   [K 445]

Once the symbolic implications of the flute and the sword are
established, the meaning of many of Kung's lines becomes clear.
Take, for instance, the following poems. In the first poem, "But no
notes can be blown on my flute-like heart" denotes the poet's reluctance to reveal his feelings in verse at the moment of parting. In
the second, "Outside of flute music in autumn lakes and hills"
represents the absence of poetic environments. In the third, "And
unsheathe our swords in a dream" means the unfolding of heroic
schemes.

Parting

To whom can I reveal my quiet grievances today?
The poets gather now like clouds, their spirits
    warm and cordial.
But no notes can be blown on my flute-like heart;
In a wind full of fallen petals I leave the south.   [K 439]

Composed in a Dream   [No. 1]

Outside of flute music in autumn lakes and hills,
There is no place in this world without sorrow.
Suddenly I hear the infinite green of the sea,
And appoint myself the little lord of the southeast.   [K 496]

On New Year's Eve in the year Hsin-ssu [1821], I passed the night at a
Taoist temple with a fellow scholar, P'eng Yün-chang; P'eng brought out his
collected poems which I spent all night reading and wrote this poem at the
back of the collection.

This also is a reflection of *karma:*
That we listen to the same stroke of the temple bell,
Light a lamp away from the sea of humanity,
And unsheathe our swords in a dream.
The whiteness of snow lightens all thought of favors
    and grievances;
Chanting poems uncovers the truth of suffering
    and emptiness.
Tomorrow morning guests will fill the hall.
Who would find traces of this past year credible?   [K 456]

II   *The Sea and the Gushing Spring*

In the poems cited in section I, we find other recurring images which warrant examination. The image of a rolling body of water occurs three times. If the flute symbolizes poetic feeling and expression, could the sea and the tide stand for the periodic upsurge of literary inspiration? After all, in two of the poems, "Autumn Thoughts [No. 1]" and "Repenting My Mind's Turmoil," the sea and the tide are actually similes of the heart/mind, *hsin*. Kung also compares one of his favorite poets, Fang Chou (1665–1701), to the bright moon and Fang's style to the billowing waves.[2] In a poem about reincarnation, Kung concludes: "By chance I find myself adrift in a sea of words,/ In my next life I shall re-edit Ting-an's poems."[3] And it may not be a simple coincidence that the line which Kung obtained in a dream prompting the completion of two poems is: "As the tide rises in the Eastern Sea, the moon shines furiously."[4] By the same token, the rather obscure "Composed in a Dream [No. 1]" translated above, with its reference to the sea's infinite green, could be about the sudden and elated awareness of the self at the stirring of poetic inspiration. The last line might signify the carefree state of being master of everything.

Closely related to this is Kung's usage of the bursting spring, a body of water sprouting from within, as a metaphor of poetic inspiration. The very first quatrain of the 315 *Miscellaneous Poems of the Year Chi-hai* begins with the lines:

> How can writing a book be compared with observing
>   the mind?
> But I can't bear the spring of overflowing words[5]
>   which gushes out at night.   [K 509]

And in one of the poems on abstaining from verse making, the tears caused by the demon of poetic inspiration are also described in terms of a gushing spring:

Abstaining From Poetry   [No. 2]

> Bitter tears erupt from my entrails,
> Gushing out at night like a spring.
> Where do these tears come from?
> Perhaps from the evil enchantment of poetry.

> Now I vow to empty this heart,
> For when the heart is empty, tears will cease.
> If something is still not extinct,
> Why keep track of it? [K 451]

What these poems reveal of Kung's attitude toward creativity and the influence of Buddhism will be clear in subsequent sections. But first we must take a look at his other major themes: dreams, childhood, and motherly love, all of which throw light on his frame of mind.

III *Dreams*

That dreams occur frequently in Kung's poems can be seen even in the several examples cited. In his collected works are poems which either came to him in their entirety during a dream,[6] or were prompted by a line which drifted into his mind during a dream, as in the two poems mentioned in section II. In the year following his first vow to abstain from writing poetry, twenty quatrains instigated by dreams were burned in an effort to halt the creation of such poems.[7] There is also a series of seven eight-line regulated poems *(lü-shih)* commemorating dreams. The content of many of these dream poems is very obscure. However, based on the way Kung treats dreams in poems not primarily concerned with the actual fact of dreaming or verse making, and in which the meaning is clearly discernible, a few observations can be made on the general flavor and implication of dreams in his poems. Take the following two quatrains, for example. The Ch'ien-lung courtiers in the first poem refer to the scholar-officials who lived in the Golden Age of the Ch'ing dynasty and therefore had the opportunity to fulfill their political ambitions. In the second poem, the concluding line alludes to the remark of Confucius in the *Analects* that he had become so old and weak he no longer dreamed of the Duke of Chou, his ideal statesman.

Desolation

> Desolate and idle we drag hopelessly on,
> Neglecting both the green hills and the green pages
>   of bamboo annals.
> Ch'ien-lung courtiers I have never met
> Drift frequently without cause into my dreams. [K 453]

Miscellaneous Poems of the Year Chi-hai [No. 63]

The Classics have schools of interpretation I always respect,
Except for *The Odes* which has no good commentary.
My mind is the same as the ancient poet's[8] mind;
I dream old, old dreams again of the Duke of Chou.   [K 515]

It becomes apparent that to Kung dreams represent a constant source of inspiration and the embodiment of ideals rather than something fleeting and unsubstantial. We can support this conclusion by viewing the above illustrations together with the previous examples of "Composed in a Dream [No. 1]," "unsheathe our swords in a dream," and "As the tide rises in the Eastern Sea, the moon shines furiously" (the line obtained in a dream which prompted two poems). In other words, Kung does not subscribe to the common notion of "a life of drunkenness and dreams" (*tsui-sheng meng-ssu*), as the popular saying goes. For that matter, drinking songs, a favorite subject among Chinese poets, are conspicuously absent in Kung's works. As he puts it,

Drinking makes others drunk, it makes me wakeful.
Difficult indeed to be forever in a carefree
   befuddled state!   [K 475]

Thus, Kung's ever-vigilant mind makes it impossible for him to succumb to a state of drunken forgetfulness. For the same reason, dreams in Kung's *shih* poems stand for a higher plane of existence; they suggest goals to be achieved, not unreality and oblivion.[9] This is further illustrated by the poems on dreams and childhood recollections introduced in the next section.

IV   *The Child Mind*

Of the goals in Kung's life, the recapturing of a childlike state of mind probably was closest to his heart. Since dreams often express his cherished ideals, many consist of childhood experiences. Kung confirms this in one of the Chi-hai poems:

Miscellaneous Poems of the Year Chi-hai [No. 170]

The joy and sorrow of my youth exceeded everyone's.
I sang and wept without cause, always sincerely.
Having grown, social life makes me muddled and shrewd;
My child mind returns only in dreams.   [K 526]

The same attempt to regain the child mind, the same contrast between the purity of childhood and the distractions of adult life, appears in poems differing considerably in imagery and mood. Note the following examples. "Frantic" in the opening line of the first poem translates one of Kung's favorite words, *k'uang*, literally "mad." Together with the abrupt change in the middle of the poem and the intensity of the lamp glow in the last line, the impression of fast-dissipating vitality distinguishes this poem from the quiet stillness of the second example. Both, however, reflect the influence of Buddhism. In the first poem, "fate" is a translation of *yüan*, a Buddhist term for causality. In the second, the meditative atmosphere of Zen permeates every line.

Sudden Recollection

Frantic study for the Examination consumes my middle years—
A fate which fell to me late in life—
Suddenly I recall my peculiar child mind.
A red lamp glows through endless time.   [K 495]

On Waking from a Nap

It doesn't resemble longing; it doesn't resemble Zen.
Waking from a dream, my eyes fill with tears.
Flowers repose in the vase and incense burns in silence;
I trace my child mind back twenty-six years.   [K 466]

Childhood experiences are closely associated with motherly love in Kung's poems. "On Waking from a Nap" was written in 1823, the year Kung's mother died. The "twenty-six years" refers to the time Kung first received poetry lessons from his mother at the age of seven.[10] The "Poems on Three Special Favorites," also written in 1823, single out Wu Wei-yeh (1609–72), Fang Chou, and Sung Ta-tsun (1746–1804) as his favorite poets; though Kung knew they were not first-rate, he liked them best because he had studied them with his mother.[11] Other poems written in memory of his mother include: "In remembrance of mother at seeing a sprig of red plum while visiting K'un-shan in the winter of the year I-yu (1825)," "Dreaming of our old house and seeing my late mother and Aunt P'an on New Year's Eve of the year I-yu," "Written at the end of a number of volumes found in a broken basket after the fire, all mother's possessions," and "Expressing my Feelings on New Year's

Day."[12] In addition, numerous references to his mother's tender care appear in poems of childhood reminiscence, e.g., "The Fa-yüan Monastery," "Verses under a Cool Moon [No. 4]," and "From Spring to Autumn: Incidental Thoughts [No. 13]."[13]

By contrast, it is interesting to note that no explicit description of Kung's feeling for his father occurs in his poems,[14] although his father, Kung Li-cheng, died only a few months before Kung in 1841. Perhaps Kung's strong attachment to his mother, from a family renowned for its scholarship, can be ascribed in part to the fact that she personally supervised his early education. From a reference in a lament for an old family friend, "My father was stern while you were unrestrained,"[15] we gather that his father was probably rather aloof and therefore not as likely to be the object of the son's affection. Whatever the reasons, the following poem fascinatingly illustrates the intimate relation between mother and son, and the almost mystical link between Kung's inner self and poetic inspiration. The note Kung wrote at the end of this poem reads: "Every time I hear the sound of a flute at sundown, I become ill. Not knowing why, I merely note the fact here."

Sending a Letter Home in Winter
During a Minor Illness

> The yellow sunlight warms half my window.
> Everywhere human noises have subsided.
> The flute of the candy seller sobs in a narrow lane,
> Its notes deep and intermittent.
> Each time I heard this sound as a child,
> My spirit was instantly entranced.
> Then my mother knew I was ill
> And covered me with a cotton quilt.
> Dreaming at night and moaning from the chill,
> I threw myself on her bosom.
> Now a full-grown man,
> This affliction persists;
> I bathe in the bounty of my mother's love
> As a man, as a child.
> This year we are far apart,
> Sitting alone beyond the horizon.
> With mind and spirit declining day by day,
> How can I hope to be completely enlightened?
> Dark and silent, silent and dark,
> Hugging my coverlet, to whom can I turn?   [K 454–55]

V *The Inner Self and Creativity*

The association between illness and inspiration recalls the previous poems on repenting the activities of the mind and abstaining from poetry. Together with the emphasis on dreams, these poems show that creativity for Kung is a purely internal process, a perpetual turmoil in the depths of his consciousness. At the same time, creativity is something to be avoided. In spite of the occasional outbursts of pride and self-satisfaction regarding his writings,[16] Kung keenly conveys the notion that talent and learning are actually a curse. His poem "Written at the end of a number of volumes found in a broken basket after the fire, all mother's possessions," begins with the lines:

> I try to trace the source of sorrows
> And find it in a pile of battered books.   [K 477]

The opening of "From Spring to Autumn: Incidental Thoughts [No. 14]" reads:

> Perilous indeed, nearly falling
> Into a deep, fathomless pit!
> I knew nothing of worries,
> But words entrapped me.   [K 488]

And the last quatrain of the medley written at the capital in 1819 sums up his effort to free himself from excessive emotions and words:

> I want to write verses which are simple and plain,
> But each time I lift my brush, I lose control of my lucid,
>   my keen feelings.
> Let me cast off the name of madman and abandon
>   all thoughts:
> Absolute silence will be my teacher.   [K 442]

This negative view toward the written and spoken word also finds expression in a larger context. The following poem, for example, stresses, in a political framework and a satirical vein, the same desire to avoid words. The Tung-hua Gate in the first line is one of the three entrances to the Imperial City.[17] The Emperor's Privy Council (*Chün-chi ch'u*) was located just beyond this gate. "New Trea-

tises" (*Hsin shu*) refers to the collection of essays by the scholar Chia
I of the Han dynasty.[18] The fourth line probably means that an
insect which is too noisy detracts from its nature.[19] The term
"feminine" in the seventh line derives from an observation in the
Taoist text *Lao tzu* which says, he who knows the male and yet
preserves what is female becomes the world's reservoir, an observation which expounds the virtues of meekness and passivity.

Words of Explanation[20]

> Seeing the many dignitaries at the Tung-hua Gate,
>   I am ashamed,
> Regretting my New Treatises of the last decade.
> Timber with crazed grain is considered diseased;
> Insects which chirp too much cannot be true to their nature.
> Shallow indulgence in chronicles brings the state no relief.
> Dare I boast of aspiring[21] to be a historian?
> Let me labor to preserve the quiet and feminine,
> So no prime minister's good sleep will be ruined.   [K 482]

In Kung's opinion, the way to be rid of the curse of talent and
creativity is to shun any entanglement with literature. In "From
Spring to Autumn: Incidental Thoughts [No. 15]," he states that
"Penitence begins with writings";[22] thus, the repeated abstentions
from writing poetry mentioned in Chapter One. Such apprehension
regarding literary involvement might well have stemmed from the
anxiety and despair caused by the complexity of his learning, on the
one hand, and by his extraordinary sensitivity on the other. But the
terminology Kung uses to express many of his ideas, the very
concept of "abstinence" (*chieh*), as well as the significance he at-
taches to the mind, point to another important factor in his thought
and poetry, namely, the influence of Buddhism.

VI *Buddhism, Confucianism, and Taoism*

Exactly when Kung became interested in Buddhism is hard to
determine since most of his early works have been lost. Buddhist
concepts appear in his early poems written around the age of
twenty-eight and twenty-nine. According to a footnote to "Miscellaneous Poems of the Year Chi-hai [No. 141]," his first teacher in
Buddhism was Chiang Yüan (1761–1838), an outstanding philologist
and a student of his maternal grandfather, Tuan Yü-ts'ai. Perhaps

Kung became acquainted with Chiang because of this connection with his grandfather. It has been observed that his interest in Buddhism greatly increased after his mother's death.[23] At any rate, the Buddhist doctrine of emptiness (*k'ung*), the illusory nature of all phenomena, undoubtedly contributed to Kung's effort to stamp out sorrow and extinguish spiritual turmoil.

As far as his poetry is concerned, Buddhist terms and imagery abound. Even the poem written at a Taoist temple on New Year's Eve (translated above at the end of section I) deals with Buddhist concepts like the *karma* of rebirth and the truth of suffering and emptiness. It should be interesting to see how Kung compares Buddhism with Confucianism and Taoism, the other mainstreams of Chinese thought, and what effect Buddhism has on his poetry.

Kung clearly states his opinion regarding the position of Buddhism in the following poem on a Sanskrit volume. The Nine Schools in ancient China refer to Confucianism, Taoism, Divination, Law, Logic, Mohism, Politics, Agriculture, and Miscellaneous. "Holy scriptures of the West" stands for Buddhist texts, not European masterpieces as some have mistakenly implied.[24] "Literary Buddha," *wen-fo*, is probably a reference to *shih-chia wen-ni*, the transliteration of Shakyamuni in Chinese.[25] Kung, however, is taking the character *wen* literally here.

Written on a Sanskrit Volume

> Confucianism was only one of the Nine Schools;
> What good is there in being a leading Confucian?
> The magnificent holy scriptures of the West
> Surpass and encompass all of them.
> Even in matters of literary style,
> These texts can be models for the Nine Schools.
> Shakyamuni is called the literary Buddha;
> Profound indeed, it weighs heavily on my thoughts.   [K 506]

Not only does Kung subordinate Confucianism to Buddhism; he also looks upon it as but one of the many schools of Chinese thought. He dwells on this opinion in the following poem. The last two lines imply a definition of the term Confucianism and a distinction between "true Confucianism" and the perverted Confucianism of later days. In other words, those who say that Confucianism was the school that died out first are referring to true Confucianism, not its namesake and corrupted residue which lives on.

From Spring to Autumn: Incidental Thoughts [No. 10]

> When the historian[26] listed the Nine Schools,
> Confucianism was only one of them;
> Each master had his own truth
> And would not follow the Confucian way.
> In later generations Confucianism became more honored
> And Confucians all the more brazen.
> In the vast empire, at court and in the country,
> There must have been more than nine schools.
> Of the Nine Schools in ancient times,
> Which are flourishing and which extinct?
> Some say Confucianism perished first:
> What could that mean?   [K 487]

Since Kung's poems on the whole are emotive rather than didactic, his admiration for the true Confucian spirit comes through not so much in the form of doctrinal statements as in the sympathy he shows for the hardships of the common people and his eagerness to do something about them. The Buddhist concept of compassion (*tz'u-pei*), of course, also contributes to this attitude. The following poems illustrate Kung's feeling for the plight of others. The last three examples belong to the Chi-hai medley. Written late in the poet's life, this medley especially reflects Kung's persistent concern for the nation and his lingering attachment to the court, both of which stem from the Confucian tradition.

Miscellaneous Poems Written in the Capital from Spring to Summer of the Year Chi-mao (1819) [No. 13]

> Doodles and scribbles crowd half my life.
> Why do I avoid fame in middle age?
> Talented men in many fields go hungry.
> Suddenly moved by compassion, I refrain from competing.
> [K 442]

Miscellaneous Poems of the Year Chi-hai [No. 21]

> I hoped to see new mulberry trees throughout the province of Chi.
> Even on a second visit I saw no clouds of green leaves.
> How much relief can a scholar's policy bring?
> Let it grieve the Weaving Maid of the south![27]   [K 510]

Miscellaneous Poems of the Year Chi-hai [No. 83]

A single hawser takes over ten men to tow,
And at least a thousand boats ply this river.
I, too, once consumed the grain of the imperial granary.[28]
Hearing the trackers' "Heave-ho!" at night, my tears pour.
                                                                        [K 517]

Miscellaneous Poems of the Year Chi-hai [No. 297]

Man's nature has always been the same.
Why sing about the remote wild goose beyond this world?[29]
Were it not for crises shared by the whole empire,
Who would understand the sympathy of Confucius?[30]
(On my trip north, my carriage overturned four times and was mired in the
mud twice. Each time I got out of my predicament with the help of
passers-by.)   [K 536]

For the sake of elaboration and additional evidence, perhaps we
should examine one more poem in which the same idea of mutual
concern for and close ties between people is expressed, though with
a surfeit of classical terms and allusions. The quotation "brothers
and companions" in the fifth line derives from an observation in the
"Western Inscription" (Hsi ming) of Chang Tsai (1020–76), a Neo-
Confucianist of Sung times. In it Chang stresses the common bond
between men and all things in the universe, saying that "The people
are my brothers, all physical objects my companions."[31] "The Four
Seas" is a general reference to the Chinese empire.[32] The widow
who burned what she was weaving alludes to a passage in the Tso
chuan [commentaries to the Spring and Autumn Annals] where a
widow was more concerned over the fall of the Chou dynasty and
the ensuing calamity than her own weaving.[33] Because of its frequent flooding, the Yellow River probably stands for the people's
hardships.[34] Western Ch'in may refer to foreign aggression, like
that of Fu Chien (A.D. 337–84) of Western Ch'in against Eastern
Chin.[35] "Think thrice" means thinking very carefully. It originates
in the story of Chi Wen-tzu in the Confucian Analects. Chi always
deliberated three times before he acted on anything. When the
Master heard about it, he said, "Twice is enough."[36] The "man of
Ch'i" is the equivalent of a worry-wart who fretted that the sky
might one day collapse.[37] The last two lines are ironical in tone and
imply the opposite of what they say.

From Spring to Autumn: Incidental Thoughts [No. 2]

> The masses are our brothers,
> The universe a neighborhood.
> Not a single hair can be pulled
> Without affecting the whole person.
> The sage's expression "brothers and companions"
> Could not possibly be an exaggeration.
> When the Four Seas turn to autumn,
> Not one room remains in spring.
> When the Chou dynasty tottered,
> The widow burned her weaving to ashes.
> That's why a patriotic, spirited scholar
> Cannot help but feel anguish.
> Gazing at the flowers I recall the Yellow River,
> Facing the moon I think of Western Ch'in.
> High dignitaries, don't think thrice,
> Consider me a man of Ch'i.   [K 485]

When we turn to Taoism, it can be said that the influence in this case is more a matter of poetic device than conviction. Familiar Taoist settings and personages, like the Jade Emperor's celestial palace, the Fairy Queen's residence at the Western Pond, and the troop of well-known immortals (*hsien*), each with its own abode, lend themselves readily to allegorical purposes. Thus, the "Ease of Travel," which is cloaked in obscure expressions and Taoist images, actually hints at the poet's preference for retirement over an official career in the capital.[38] Advocacy of retirement is also elaborated in "A Song to Recruit the Recluses by the Immortal at the T'ung River." Though much more comprehensible, this poem is also steeped in Taoist imagery, as its title clearly indicates.[39] Another poem with a great number of Taoist terms is "Distinguishing Immortals." Here the immortals stand for government officials, and the poet is trying to differentiate the true from the pretended.[40] Taoist images also serve as a major poetic device in the "Song on the Immortal Butterflies at the Bureau of Sacrifices." As explained in its prose introduction, this is a song that praises the vice-minister of that bureau while underscoring the lack of appreciation for such an upright person.[41]

In addition, there are the poems on dreams, the short lyrics on celestial journeys, and many of Kung's love *tz'u* which also make use of Taoist conventions to allegorize political or personal issues. Some of these *tz'u* will be taken up in Chapter Five. The short lyrics on celestial journeys will be discussed in the next chapter in connection with Kung's method of presentation. The point to be made here is that the Taoist concepts which appear in Kung's poems derive either from the amazingly broad scope of his knowledge, or from the stock ideas which had already been absorbed into the mainstream of Chinese thought and were therefore shared by all educated people. They do not represent any fundamental intellectual commitment. Such a commitment belongs to Buddhism.

VII   *The Religious and the Romantic*

Besides being the bedrock of Kung's intellectual orientation, Buddhism also characterizes his poetry through a typical fusion with romantic subject matters. The quatrain on "The Lung-ching Monastery at Hangchow," for instance, begins with a quiet monastic mood which develops into a sudden ending of mad abandonment. "Meditation" and "flower" represent two of Kung's favorite subjects, one pointing to spiritual enlightenment, the other to romantic adventures.

> The red clay pavilion has collapsed and visitors seldom come.
> The sounds of bell and chime rise solemnly from the blue-green
>   mountain.
> To dwell in meditation is not my lot, so I violate the rules
> And steal a monastery flower home.   [K 447]

That these two apparently contradictory aspects of life are often blended in Kung's poems can further be illustrated in two quatrains entitled "Last Night." "Rebirth" in the first example registers "Three Lives" (*san-sheng*), a popular Buddhist term that refers to a being's past, present, and future incarnations, implying transmigration of the soul as well as the law of causality or *karma*. "Hairpins and bracelets," on the other hand, is a common metaphor for women in Chinese literature. In the second poem, the expression "subtle and wondrous truth" (*wei-miao fa*) and the conclusion following it are both Buddhist in nature, while "flowers" and "seeds of sorrow" remind us of Kung's romantic attachments.

Last Night [No. 1]

Last night's river tide has not ebbed.
A boat passenger lying by a window ponders rebirth.
He hears the medicine pot, which seems to boil—
Nothing like the sounds of hairpins and bracelets
    from neighbors to the east.[42]

Last Night [No. 2]

Planting flowers is planting the seeds of sorrow.
But without flowering branches I am heartbroken.
Recently I learned a most subtle and wondrous truth:
To see flowers as shadows which leave no traces.   [K 448]

In one of Kung's poems to his wife, Buddhist terms have also been fused with warm sentiment. Judging by the fourth line, the couple probably had had a quarrel or some misunderstanding. "The moon dropped into your breast" indicates that she was pregnant.[43] "Chance" translates *huan yüan*, or illusory causality, a term referring to this world's causal relations which are actually unreal when viewed in the greater context of cosmic principles or *dharma*. "Flowers in heaven" may allude to the lotus which, in the paradise of the Pure Land, symbolizes blessings and spiritual achievement, though perhaps it falls short of representing a high enough enlightenment for Kung. Other Buddhist images and concepts include Zen, Sutra, incense, penitence (*ch'an*), and boundless *dharma*. Characteristically, they are mingled with emotive elements like "deep concern," "blooming years," and the tenderness of the poem as a whole.

Post-House Drum [No. 3]

Your letter full of deep concern made me see your virtue.
I wish to end my frivolity and slowly turn to Zen.
Household cares have long eroded your inner brilliance.
Do not let misunderstanding mar your blooming years.
Watching for flowers in heaven, you pray for commonplace
    blessings.
The moon dropped into your breast, leave the outcome to chance.
With a golden Sutra and a stick of incense,
I pray in penitence for you and for me, since *dharma*
    is boundless.   [K 444]

Sometimes the religious and the romantic are blended only in the conclusion of a poem rather than all through it, as in the following example written to the same rhyme words of a friend's poem. The first two lines introduce the poet's experience and accomplishment. The next two lines most likely symbolize the courtiers' unawareness of the impending downfall of the dynasty and the unwise reliance on worthless officials. The fifth and sixth lines pertain to the poet and his inability to flatter and please the authorities, unlike the way concubines and flowers can. The concluding lines tell of his wish for seclusion at a far-off place where he could spend the rest of his life in the company of beautiful women and Buddhist scriptures.

Written on the Wall of an Inn, to the Rhyme
of Chou Po-t'ien [I-wei]

I have infinite experience at the examination centers.
My all-embracing "Heart's History"[44] is unique.
The autumn air does not startle the swallows in the hall.
The setting sun lingers lovingly over the roadside crows.
The widow in the neighboring house to the east[45] is too
    old to be a concubine.
This ancient tree with its pervading roots can hardly rival
    a flower.
When may I follow the far-off flight of the wild goose[46]
And bury my remaining years in beautiful women and Buddhist
    scriptures?   [K 449–50]

From a poetic point of view, such a combination of emotive and intellectual elements helps prevent the former from becoming trite and the latter from drifting into flat abstractions. From a philosophical point of view, joining the romantic and the religious reflects the influence of Zen, or Ch'an, a discipline which not only transcends rationality and every polarity, but sees enlightenment even in the commonplace and the absurd. It may be appropriate to end this chapter with a poem which, in addition to summarizing Kung's lifelong occupations and interests, embraces his hope for spiritual emancipation. At the instant of enlightenment, contradictions become resolved, aesthetics and action unite, while the religious and the romantic merge.

Sitting at Night [No. 2]

Dark, dark thoughts from every direction fill my mind,
As I glance at the empire void of talent.
Only in maturity do I share the historian's calling,[47]
For in my youth I stumbled into abstruse philosophies.[48]
Beyond a high military appointment and the quest for immortality,
My talent dissipates in entwining emotions and intoxicating zeal.
If by chance the Zen barrier is smashed—
A person beautiful as jade, a sword like a rainbow.   [K 467]

CHAPTER 3

Secrets Unlocked:
Kung's Method of Presentation

> Every word in your verses stems from loyalty
>   and filial piety,
> Despite the display of Buddhism and misty images;
> For through strangeness you reveal the plain
>   and substantial—
> Do not scold me for unlocking your secrets!
>   —Yang Hsiang-chi, "On Reading Mr. Ting-an's
>   Collected Works" [K 638]

ALTHOUGH the above observation of Yang Hsiang-chi (1825–78) is debatable with regard to the degree of significance of Buddhism to Kung, it does show how prominent the flavor of strangeness is in his poems and rightly sees in this strangeness a disguise for his social and political concerns. This chapter will examine the characteristics of Kung's poetry, deemphasizing the incomprehensible and the mechanical. Needless to say, the sum total of these representative features still falls short of his poetry as a whole, nor can we generalize any single feature and expect it to be true of all his poems. His Chi-hai quatrains and *tz'u* lyrics, for example, differ sufficiently from his other verse forms to merit separate coverage. They will be discussed in subsequent chapters.

I *Chickens and Dogs of the Immortal Household*

The first thing of note in Kung's method of presentation is his fondness for metaphor. The poem "Written on the Wall of an Inn, to the Rhyme of Chou Po-tien" (translated in section VII above) illustrates this characteristic. No natural image in this poem, be it autumn air, swallows, the setting sun, crows, an ancient tree, a flower, or the wild goose, is included for its own sake. Each is metaphorical: "autumn air" stands for the dynasty's impending downfall; "swallows in the hall" for the courtiers in their sheltered environment; the "setting sun" for the declining dynasty; "roadside crows" for unworthy officials; an "ancient tree" for the poet himself; "flower" for showy characters; and the "wild goose" for seclusion. Kung's skill lies in his ability to weld ideas as well as mood and imagery into a cohesive whole. The broad sweep of words like "infinite" and "all-embracing" corresponds to the distant flight of the wild goose, while "autumn air," "setting sun," "widow . . . old," and "ancient tree" associate harmoniously with one another, forming a somber picture of imminent doom. The cloistered frailty of "swallows in the hall," the vagabond coarseness of "roadside crows," the subjugation and flattery implied in "concubine," and the coquettishness suggested by "flower" attest to the poet's appropriate choice of objects. Even single words like "startle" and "lingers" fit so well in the overall message that any substitution would surely damage the effect. The poetic mastery illustrated in these eight lines is overwhelming if we further take into consideration the following points: the close resemblance of this poem to Kung's own life (in other words, that this is not a concocted situation); the *lü-shih* regulations regarding parallelism and tone pattern which it has to observe;[1] and the fact that the rhyme scheme conforms to a poem written by someone else.

Kung employs metaphors most frequently when dealing with public issues, as in the present poem, probably because direct expressions might result in censorship. After he had failed the examination for a position in the emperor's Privy Council in 1821, he wrote a cycle of fifteen "Short Lyrics on Travels in the Immortals' Realm" (*Hsiao yu-hsien tz'u*) to ridicule high officialdom by means of allegories on the immortal world. On the surface these read like elegant lyrics on an intriguing rendezvous. However, once the central theme is revealed, each becomes a masterpiece of subdued irony and satire. Notice, for example, the following three selections from the series.[2] In the first poem, "refining cinnabar," a common practice among Taoists, represents Kung's repeated attempts to pass the metropolitan examination. "The *luan* and crane" are constant companions of a Taoist. "Bypassing the Isle of Immortals" refers to

his detour around the metropolitan examination and the Han-lin
Academy by taking the examination for the Privy Council as a short
cut to high office. In the second poem, "chickens and dogs" mocks
the scholars who, having passed the examination, turn their backs
on former friends and behave as ludicrously in their esteemed
positions as animals wearing gorgeous garments and parroting
human words. "The Huai Prince" is the Prince of Huai-nan who,
according to the *Biographies of Immortals (Shen-hsien chuan)*,
ascended to heaven in broad daylight. The chickens and dogs in his
residence happened to peck at the musical instruments he had left
behind, and they too attained immortality.[3] In the third poem, "the
heavenly roster" refers to the names of successful candidates. "The
sisters" probably stands for fellow scholars. Ts'ang Chieh in the last
line was supposed to be the inventor of writing at the time of the
legendary Yellow Emperor. Here, Kung jeers at the fact that he
failed even the examination for the Privy Council merely because
his handwriting was considered inappropriate by the examiners.

Short Lyrics on Travels in the Immortals' Realm [No. 1]

> Through countless calamities in refining cinnabar,
>   the Way is not fulfilled;
> In an ethereal wind, the *luan* and crane complain
>   of their destiny.
> Who pointed out that celestial route
> Which bypasses the Isle of Immortals and reaches
>   the other shore?

Short Lyrics on Travels in the Immortals' Realm [No. 10]

> The chickens and dogs of the immortal household
>   have grown fat recently,
> They no longer fly to the old home of the Huai Prince,
> But squat on golden couches babbling human words,
> Wear heavenly garments sitting on high seats, and
>   turn their backs on humans.

Short Lyrics on Travels in the Immortals' Realm [No. 11]

Pondering the heavenly roster, I linger long:
We all wrote on the same paper woven from the same cocoons.
The sisters advise me to practice human script
And stop resenting that Ts'ang Chieh was not of immortal caliber.

[K 458–59]

Again, a unified atmosphere and interrelated images weld these quatrains into an articulate whole. At the same time, we find a delightful sense of humor which lightens the underlying sarcasm and bitterness. Such a transformation of common, practical subjects into interesting, lyrical expressions further testifies to Kung's poetic skill and creativity.

In addition to poems written in the "celestial journey," or *yu-hsien* style,[4] instances of metaphorical presentation occur in many other poems to be discussed. Suffice it here to examine one more illustration because of the popularity it has enjoyed and the poignancy of its metaphors:

On Historical Events

Golden powder filled the fifteen southeastern prefectures;
Ten thousand layers of favors and wrongs on men of letters.
Lechers of the Salt Ministry[5] held complete control;
Palace ladies with round fans occupied high positions.
Scholars rose fearfully from their mats at the mention
    of literary inquisition;
They wrote books only for a living.
Where are T'ien Heng and his five hundred followers now?
Had they returned, do not tell me they would all
    be awarded noble ranks!   [K 471]

It is very common in Chinese poetry to criticize political events of the reigning dynasty under the title of "On Historical Events" (*Yung-shih*) in order to avoid persecution. The question is what Kung was criticizing. It has been suggested that this is a satire of the officialdom of his time. "Golden powder" refers to the lead powder used in women's cosmetics in those days. "Men of letters" were therefore compared to glamorous women who concerned themselves only with good looks and the ability to please. Political power lodged in the hands of lavish, irresponsible administrators of the salt monopoly. Important offices were filled by courtiers who flattered the emperor like "palace ladies." Scholars without official posts feared censorship so much that they produced books just to maintain a livelihood. As a warning to those who desired to serve the government, the conclusion alludes to T'ien Heng and his five hundred followers who committed suicide rather than serve another ruler under the then newly established Han dynasty. In other words, the central message of the poem is taken to be an admonition of submitting to the Ch'ing court.[6]

Such an anti-Manchu interpretation has been questioned, however, on the gound that Kung himself was very keen on serving the Ch'ing dynasty. Moreover, this very poem was written in 1826, after he had tried repeatedly to pass the metropolitan examination.[7] Wu Ch'ang-shou, in his chronological biography of Kung, mentions a separate episode which might have prompted the poem. Tseng Yü (1760–1831),[8] a salt commissioner, refused to bribe another official who happened to pass by Yangchow. The latter retaliated by sending Tseng a poem containing the lines "Appointing talented men out of order is the business of the enlightened ruler;/ Seeking enjoyment in his declining years expresses the feeling of an old minister"; he also circulated copies of it. Since these lines could be interpreted as criticism of the emperor for failing to promote Tseng, they resulted in Tseng's dismissal when word reached the emperor. Although this incident had been transmitted orally and therefore might not be reliable,[9] it throws light on the meaning of Kung's poem and cautions against too radical an interpretation of Kung as well.

Judging from the content of the poem, there is no reason why, at least on one level, its title cannot be taken literally. The historical events in the poem may well refer to the relationship between the early Ch'ing court and the surviving scholar-officials of the previous Ming dynasty. The southeast felt the pressure most not only because of the number of scholars in that area but also because of the Manchu policy of discrimination against native Chinese, especially those from the provinces of Kiangsu and Chekiang.[10] At the same time, the early Ch'ing emperors did impose severe literary censorship on the one hand and, on the other, sponsored scholarly projects which were politically harmless or ideologically useful. This fits the observations in lines five and six. The reference to T'ien Heng in the conclusion also closely parallels the predicament of the Ming survivors, or *i-lao*. Of course, such a historical comment usually reflects upon existing conditions. The point is, rather than admonishing against cooperation with the Ch'ing dynasty, Kung was actually complaining about the lack of opportunity for people like him to serve. The allusion to T'ien Heng means that outstanding men of the character of T'ien and his followers would not be appreciated even if they were available, while worthless salt administrators and coquettish courtiers were given full rein. "Lechers" with reference to the salt administrators is a translation of *hsia-k'o,* literally patrons at a brothel. Together with "ten thousand layers" of "golden powder" and "palace ladies with round fans," this word effects a cutting derision of the prostitute-like scholar-officials in general. Thus, with one stroke, Kung demonstrates his superb handling of metaphors with both historical accuracy and contemporary relevance.

II Bursting into Endless Profusion

Another characteristic of Kung's method of presentation is hyperbole, both in individual terms and in the embellishment of overall effects. Take, for instance, the "Repenting My Mind's Turmoil" translated in Chapter Two. From the outset, the fire of world destruction is introduced to exaggerate the sweeping ferocity of the poet's mental vigor. His life is then portrayed as a corrosion of energy day and night. The sword and the flute suggest the extremes of fervor and quietude. Summarily, all mental activities are considered the roots of spiritual ills, and the word "mind" (*hsin*) is repeated three times in the same line to accentuate this point. The conclusion is as relentless as the beginning of the poem: writings which inflame must in turn be destroyed by fire.

Though Kung's poems are usually not very long, several exceptions do exist. One is "Song of Rejuvenation" (*Neng ling-kung shao-nien hsing*).[11] Because of its length, this poem offers a convenient illustration of how Kung sometimes achieves a deliberately exaggerated effect by sheer accumulation. The theme itself is simple. As indicated in its short preface, this poem expresses Kung's longing for a carefree life away from politics and influential people. Out of a total of seventy-six lines, eight consecutive lines describe his intellectual goals. The nineteen lines which follow soar into a flight of the imagination; this is achieved by the familiar technique of a distant journey on which he encounters various fascinating sights, personages, and objects. The poet then daydreams about his life as a country squire, his daily pastimes, acquaintances, and the many pleasures in living close to nature: thirty-seven lines in one breath. The rolling rhythm is enhanced by the use of similar rhymes throughout.

One of Kung's longer representative poems demonstrates his lavish diction and imagery:

A Song on the Fallen Petals in West Country

Preface

One mile outside the Feng-i Gate[12] are eighty to ninety cherry-apple trees each measuring about ten spans of the hand in circumference. Because the place was too crowded with horses and carriages when the flowers were in bloom, I did not go there. On the 26th of the third month, there was a very strong wind. The next day, it subsided a bit. Thus I went out of the city to drink there with Chin Ying-ch'eng, a staff member on the Board of Rites; Wang T'an, a Second-degree Graduate; Chu Tsu-ku, a student of the Imperial College; and my younger brother Tzu-ku. This poem resulted from that outing.

The fallen petals in West Country are a wonder of the world.
Yet since ancient times only sad songs have been written
    on spring's passage.
The moment the horses and carriages depart from West Country,
Mr. Kung brings wine and comes to admire the flowers.
People did not know when he communed with spring;
But now that he sees spring off, the people laugh.
He found a few friends who would accompany him;
As they emerge from the city, their faces change color
    and their spirits are stunned by the sight:
It is like the huge tides at Ch'ien-t'ang roaring into night;
Like the battle of K'un-yang,[13] troops scattered everywhere
    at dawn;
Like eighty-four thousand goddesses[14] washing the rouge from their
    faces onto this spot.
Strange dragons and phoenixes love to roam,
Why did the carp of Ch'in Kao want to go to heaven?
The palace of the Jade Emperor is empty as though drained;
In the thirty-six heavens[15] there is not one beautiful girl.
It is also like Mr. Kung's worries and troubles:
Strange oddities bursting into endless profusion.
He exhausted the *Tripitaka*[16] in his studies,
And is especially fond of the *Vimalakirti Sutra*
    with its lucid expressions.[17]
He has also heard that Paradise lies under four inches of fallen petals;
Closing his eyes and imagining it entrances him all the more.
But the Paradise of the West is not accessible,
Why write on and on in such flowery language?
How can these trees have endless flowers, how rain again petals fresh
    and beautiful,
So that all three hundred and sixty days can be the season of falling
    petals?   [K 488–89]

Witness the accumulation of analogies: the fallen petals are compared to tidal waves, scattered troops, the rouge of goddesses, mythological creatures, female deities, and the distresses of the poet. These analogies are held together either by similar qualities, such as being associated with heaven, or by the repetition of the word "like." Aside from this piling up of images, the effect of deliberate exaggeration can also be accounted for by individual expressions like "a wonder of the world," "empty as though drained," and "bursting into endless profusion." The last two lines of the poem in particular are exaggerative not only in ideas but also in line length; one has thirteen characters, the other ten, as against the usual seven. In addition, the flavor of nonconformity suggested by rejoicing in spring's passage rather than lamenting it sets the tone of wonder and surprise, while the comment on people's unawareness and banality hints at the poet's pride in being different. Perhaps he may even be comparing himself to the fallen petals and the analogous dragons and phoenixes which are "strange" and "love to roam." This throws light on the meaning of the allusion to Ch'in Kao's carp. Ch'in Kao was a man of late Chou times. According to legend, he had entered a river to pursue a dragon and emerged from it riding on a red carp.[18] There was also the common belief that a fish which had struggled upstream at a place called Dragon Gate changed into a dragon.[19] Thus a carp going upward to heaven connotes success and advancement. Could Kung be making a sly remark on those who aspire to high rank?

Another lengthy poem illustrating Kung's lavish imagery, and also his attitude toward people in high positions, as well as his method of exaggeration, is "Thoughts Written During a Storm on the Twentieth Night of the Tenth Month":

> The Wind God of Western Mountain,[20] haughty and cruel,
> Roars like a drunken tiger, speeds like wheels;
> Smashing the fortress, toppling the pass, he suddenly
>   sweeps in—
> Overnight the price of charcoal rises to a thousand strings.
> South of the city, I sit motionless through the night,
> Sad at heart when there is no storm.
> A letter from home arrived the night before,
> I was remembered, a fish in the human sea.
> At this moment, mother sits close to the lamp,
> Guiding her daughter-in-law, both toil-worn.

At the fourth beat of the cold night drum, they dream
    that I arrive,
Saying it is a long time since I have shared their hardships.
The letter is vague and does not tell everything;
In my uncertain fantasy, I seem to hear their groans.
Having just feasted and talked with leaders
    of the Hundred Schools,
I now sober up and my insights are true.
Overnight a lord slanders me,
Like the Wind God, infinitely haughty.
My life is a series of jolting advances and retreats;
Questioning myself, I know the reason:
A body dwelling in the universe, I am by nature solitary;
The more so for my impetuous spirit and innocence.
Reckless jesting shakes the whole hall,
This alone is enough to anger the dignitaries.
A famous name arouses slander, but not in my case;
I wish to please my parents by self-criticism.
I shall choke back any belching discontent;
Dare I imitate the earth's wild wind to vent my anger?
The lamp dies out as I rise to write these words;
A cat shivers and huddles near the curtains.
Could I return home, I would be there already,
In a crisp wind and gentle rain—spring south of the
    Yangtze. [K 463]

The Wind God literally storms into the picture from the very
beginning of the poem. It creates a powerful impact for several
reasons: the personification in the first line, the graphic similes in
the second, the magnitude and suddenness portrayed in the third,
and the dreary consequence in the fourth, additionally supporting
the term "cruel." In the rest of the poem, the effect of many images
is heightened by means of contrast. "A fish" is contrasted with
"human sea," and "a body" with "the universe," to amplify the
poet's isolation. This isolation in turn offers a contrast to "feasting
and talking with leaders of the Hundred Schools" and "reckless
jesting shaking the whole hall," two exaggerations which make the
solitary state seem all the more lonely by comparison. Then the
discontent which the poet has to swallow is more keenly felt when
contrasted with the earth's freedom to vent itself; the dying lamp
and the shivering cat give a more winterly impression when contrasted with the wind and rain of spring; at the same time the

concluding reference to the south contrasts with the storm in the north mentioned at the outset, thus sharpening the vividness of the two scenes and tightening the structure of the poem.

III   *Yearning to Become a Cloud*

In the poem just cited, we see another characteristic method of Kung: the blurring of reality and imagination. The lines beginning with "at this moment" give the impression that the poet was directly observing the activities of his mother and wife. He goes on to describe a dream (without specifying whether it was the mother's or the wife's), as though it had been enacted before his eyes. In other words, the dream, portrayed as a vision within a vision, is presented on the same plane as the factual statements in the poem. He deals with the physical phenomenon of the storm itself only in the first three lines.

Similar fusion of the real and the imaginary worlds is found in "Autumn Thoughts [No. 1]," translated in Chapter Two. The last two lines can be a portrayal of the actual starlit sky or, like the preceding "icy sword" and "flute songs," may represent only a picture in the poet's mind, symbolic of his own decline amid the dazzling successes of others.

The third poem in this cycle of three illustrates the same fusion:

Autumn Thoughts [No. 3]

The object of my thought, oh! where is it?
The wondrous spirit in my breast yearns to become
    a cloud.
The raft crossing the Milky Way[21] has little distance
    to travel;
Earth corrodes the cold flower—here again
    at this grave.
A certain river, a certain hill: your name, lost;
One hairpin, one pendant: your slightest trace
    also gone.
Rising to look beyond the towers and terraces
    silhouetted sharply,
Perhaps that elegant autumn star is you.   [K 479]

Here, the grave and its desolate surroundings are as likely to be products of the imagination as actual sights. "Cold flower" can be taken literally as fallen petals or figuratively as the remains of a woman. The visionary atmosphere touched off by the very first line, "The object of my thought . . . ," is enhanced by ethereal images like "wondrous spirit," "clouds," and "a raft crossing the Milky Way," which probably refer to the close connection between the living and the dead. The vagueness of "a certain river, a certain hill" and the intangibility suggested by "lost" and "gone" add further to the unearthly quality of the poem. Even the more definite towers, terraces, and autumn star in the conclusion may be taken as things the poet expects to see should he rise up and look, rather than what he really sees. As a matter of fact, since there are two settings in this poem, the graveside and the grounds of the towers and terraces, we cannot be sure which site is real.

Another example of the trance-like merging of reality and imagination is "Sitting at Night [No. 1]":

> Sitting sadly by a painted screen on a spring night,
> I let my eyes roam the distant sky:
> A mountain towers above the jealous hills,
> All sounds are hushed in the divine light of
>   the Emperor Star;[22]
> On the border the propitious air of heroines[23]
>   seems to rise,
> In the south the Constellation of Scholars[24]
>   has long fallen.
> Having never saved any "Queries to Heaven,"[25]
> I invite the moon to hear my poem.   [K 467]

Again, the mountain, hills, star, propitious air, and the moon can all be either objects the poet actually sees or projections of his mind. We assume there must be a window that allows him to look into the sky, but the broad scope of the sights depicted makes us wonder whether the scene is imagined or real. The fact that the poet was sitting by a painted screen also provides the physical framework necessary to seeing visions, as though he were in meditation and pondering these images in his mind. The whole poem is suffused with a peculiar illumination which seems to come partly from the heavenly bodies and partly from clairvoyance.

A final illustration of this phenomenon in Kung's poems is the following "Verses under a Cool Moon [No. 1]" which he wrote when his wife was with him in Peking. The sights in the southeast, while only imaginary, were portrayed as though they lay directly before the poet's eyes. Blurring the real and the imagined, the near at hand and the distant, produces an even more obvious effect in the Chinese text, where all but two of the pronouns in the translation are omitted and the verbs have no future tense.

Verses under a Cool Moon   [No. 1]

> Rising at night to view the rivers and hills,
> We share the flooding light of the moon.
> What hill is this, so green?
> What river is this, so clear?
> In the quiet, quiet southeastern area,
> There seems to be a house for our retirement.
> We look far toward the southeast;
> Our hearts linger on the road to Hangchow.
> Though we have no home in the city,
> We have graves outside it.
> So let us buy a mound,
> And stay near our native soil.
> I shall dismiss all worldly concerns,
> You will nurse your quiescence.
> Within a hundred *li* of our boat,
> The graveside trees should be in view.
> Facing southward to say these words,
> We almost want to fly away.   [K 481]

As discussed in Chapter Two, Kung often writes about dreams and reminiscences, turning to his inner self rather than to the outer world for inspiration. Perhaps this explains his indulgence in metaphor and symbol rather than in concrete description of external objects. It may also help explain the blurring of the distinction between the physical world and the world of imagination dealt with in this section.

IV   *Fierce Tigers of the Eastern Mountain*

Of Kung's salient features, strangeness (*ch'i* or *kuai*) is probably the most frequently mentioned. This, of course, is closely related to the hidden meanings and obscure metaphors of some of his poems. Take, for example, the "Ease of Travel" mentioned in Chapter Two in connection with the role of Taoism in his poetry. From the outset the reader is confronted with the following enigmatic lines:

> The fierce tigers of the eastern mountain
>   do not eat men.
> The fierce tigers of the western mountain
>   eat men.
> The fierce tigers of the southern mountain
>   eat men.
> The fierce tigers of the northern mountain
>   do not devour men.   [K 440]

Similar incomprehensibility occurs in poems like "Song on a Calf" and "Conversation between a Slave and a Servant-Boy."[26] Lacking a specific understanding of each and every line, we can only guess at the general implications of these poems.

Additionally, there are stylistic reasons which account for the impression of strangeness, especially in poems written in the Ancient Style (*ku-t'i shih*). The most obvious feature is line length. Rather than predominantly four-, five-, or seven-character lines, as is usually the case, we find strikingly irregular line lengths in many of the obscure poems mentioned. In "Conversation between a Slave and a Servant-Boy," for example, the lines range from two to fourteen characters, with as many four-character and five-character as seven-character lines. Although such irregularity is considered an accepted practice in *ku-t'i shih*, it does produce an effect of nonconformity when accompanied by the obscurity of the poem.

Another factor contributing to the unusual flavor of Kung's *ku-t'i shih* is the prosaic nature of his lines. With their prose syntax, particles (*hsü-tzu*), and relaxed rhythm, some of these lines read like prose statements. Even in lines of the regular length of five or seven characters, Kung often deviates from the conventional phrase divisions of, say, 2:3 and 4:3, and pauses after the first character instead. This also adds to the prosaic effect. In many cases, the single justification by traditional standards for including such lines in a poem is that their last words comply with the rhyme scheme.

Kung also likes repetition. The four lines cited at the outset of this section illustrate this tendency in his *ku-t'i shih*. So does "Abstaining from Poetry [No. 2]" discussed in Chapter Two. There, the character *mieh* (translated variously as "empty," "cease," and "extinct") is repeated three times in lines six and seven. The same characteristic recurs in his poems in the Contemporary Style (*chin-t'i shih*). In "Repenting My Mind's Turmoil," for instance, the character *hsin*, for "mind" or "mental," is repeated three times in the same line—a rather uncommon practice in Chinese poetry, though it occurs quite often in Kung's poems. Together with the amazingly frequent appearance of the character "one" (*i*), such repetition gives his verse an eccentricity which recalls his unconventional temperament.

In this connection, the extraordinary diction and imagery of some of Kung's poems must also be mentioned. We find further evidence of his calculated "madness" in such lines as "Wronged! Wronged! Truly dragons and snakes are coiling in my throat" in "Ease of Travel"; "Riotous dreams of ghosts wrangling over literature" in "Observing my Mind"; and "I can also give to a dog the horn of the unicorn from the mountain in the great wilderness" in "Conversation between a Slave and a Servant-Boy."[27]

At the same time, an archaic flavor marks many of Kung's poems. This may be explained partly by the stylistic features examined above. The prosaic phrasing, the frequent repetition of words and expressions, and the preponderance of particles (for instance, in "Verses under a Cool Moon [No. 4]," six consecutive lines end with the particle *chih*) all contribute to an unhewn plainness typical of archaism. In addition, Kung is very fond of "reduplicated words" (*tieh-tzu*), an accumulation of which also tends to have an archaizing effect. "The Fa-yüan Monastery," mentioned in Chapter Two, employs six pairs of *tieh-tzu* in a row. From a biographical standpoint, the fact that Kung was an ardent philologist and paleographer may account for the many archaic words in his writings. Furthermore, his familiarity with ancient history enabled him to draw on historical allusions at will. The "Song of a Scholar of the Han Dynasty" (*Han-ch'ao ju-sheng hsing*), for example, conveys the illusion that it pertains to antiquity even though it actually deals with the contemporary world.

Finally, in the Ancient and Contemporary styles alike, the repeated occurrence of dreams is one further explanation for the effect of strangeness in Kung's poems. As observed by Cleanth Brooks in *The Well Wrought Urn*, "A dream has an extraordinary kind of vividness often associated with strong emotional coloring. It frequently represents familiar objects, even homely ones, but with the familiarity gone and the objects endowed with strangeness. But the dream is elusive, it cannot be dissected and analyzed."[28] This passage can be applied to Kung's poetry word for word, be it a matter of strangeness, vividness, emotional coloring, or elusiveness.

Or, to quote the remarks of the Chinese scholar Liang Ch'i-ch'ao with reference to the verse of the late T'ang poet Li Shang-yin (812–58), "What he talks about is beyond my concern. If you ask me to explain it line by line, I cannot even tell you the surface meaning. But I feel that it is beautiful. When I read it, my spirit finds a new and refreshing joy. For beauty has many sides, and beauty is mysterious."[29] "Mysterious beauty" is as appropriate a description of Kung's poetry as of Li's.

V *Sorrow in My Shiny Black Hair*

The last feature of Kung's poetry to be considered is his highly personal approach which spans the divisions of subject matter and method of presentation. Lest his romantic adventures discussed in Chapter One leave the impression that Kung was just an irresponsible reveler, let us first turn to the cycle of "Post-House Drum" written to his wife. Kung married twice. His first wife, a granddaughter of Tuan Yü-ts'ai, died in 1813 after one year of marriage. Two years later, Kung married his second wife, surnamed Ho. From the "Verses under a Cool Moon [No. 1]," translated in section III, we gather that she must have been quite an understanding woman, one able to share her husband's frustration and desire for seclusion. In the three poems in this cycle, Kung expresses a sincere appreciation of her forbearance as well as the wish to repent his intemperate ways so that they could lead a quieter life together. Though the third poem has already been examined in Chapter Two, it is quoted again below to illustrate the continuity in the poet's thought and feeling.

Post-House Drum

River lights, post-house drum, frost fills the sky;
A brief dream, gently sweet, ruffles this traveler's feelings.
Night deepens as plum blossoms cast shadows on silken
    curtains;
Herbs in a silver kettle emit fragrance in the spring chill.
My mother's illness lessens, her letters come frequently;
Our son's studies conclude, the days gradually lengthen.
I wish to cast off the sorrow of separation for a moment,
But the stitches of your sewing are here in my clothing.
    . . .

> Hairpins fill the high tower, lamplight fills
>   the city;
> Flowers swaying in the wind[30] cannot help their
>   unbridled flirting;
> I use them to siphon off my vitality on a long journey,
> How can a minor tune jar a major key?
> People scoff at the premature sorrow in my shiny black hair;
> My squandering gold away without cause makes them angry.
> The myriad affairs of my life strain both heart and mind—
> But marrying a madman begets poor *karma*.
>   . . .
> Your letter full of deep concern made me see your virtue.
> I wish to end my frivolity and slowly turn to Zen.
> Household cares have long eroded your inner brilliance.
> Do not let misunderstanding mar your blooming years.
> Watching for flowers in heaven, you pray for commonplace
>   blessings.
> The moon dropped into your breast, leave the outcome to
>   chance.
> With a golden Sutra and a stick of incense,
> I pray in penitence for you and for me, since *dharma*
>   is boundless.   [K 443–44]

Like the above cycle, most of Kung's poems are self-expressions rather than narratives; they reveal the poet's own thoughts and feelings rather than document the development of events. Even such a rare exception as the "Song of a Scholar of the Han Dynasty," which comments on the various aspects of Ch'ing history in the guise of a Han setting, begins with a biographical account of the poet.[31] Moreover, the poem is so filled with obscurity and subjective viewpoints that it stands apart from the social and political portraits of a Tu Fu or a Po Chü-i. This does not mean that Kung's poems are necessarily restricted in their appeal. On the contrary, what distinguishes him as a poet is his ability to present his personal experiences on a universal level, to turn the one facet of reality which he encounters—be it a vase of flowers, the boat-trackers by the river, or a carriage mired in the mud—into a prismatic reflection of the whole human situation.

Because Kung usually has this larger context in mind, his personal poems often contain a socio-political relevance. Thus, his poem commenting on the fact that he only started trends but never

taught, reveals the low status of scholars who had no official position. The dual emphasis on aesthetics and action in his poems often
relates closely to political developments in the southeast and
northwest. And his poems on romantic adventures and Buddhist
pursuits delineate the frustration of many a minor official.

In the opinion of the Ch'ing critic Wu Ch'iao (17th cent.), "A
poem should contain the poet's personality";[32] or as the poet Chang
Wen-t'ao (1764–1814) put it, "A poem without the self is best
deleted;/Ten thousand of them piled on a bed would still be nothing."[33] Kung's poetry certainly meets this criterion. Whether he is
speaking in metaphor or hyperbole, on the realistic or imaginary
level, and irrespective of the plainness or strange obscurity of his
language, Kung's personality always lurks behind the lines.
Furthermore, he has so successfully fused the personal with the
socio-political that his poems echo not only his own voice but also
that of his age in general.

CHAPTER 4

Songs of a Fallen Petal: The Chi-hai Quatrains

My sorrow at parting swells as the sun begins to set.
The instant my horse heads eastward I reach the horizon.
Petals fall but not without feeling,
Becoming spring soil to nurture flowers again.
—Miscellaneous Poems of the Year Chi-hai   [No. 5, K 509]

A S mentioned in Chapter One, section VI, Kung resigned his office at the capital and returned to his native city of Hangchow in the year Chi-hai, 1839. On his way south he wrote a medley of 315 seven-character quatrains (*chüeh-chü*) known as the *Miscellaneous Poems of the Year Chi-hai (Chi-hai tsa-shih)*. The poet recollected a year later: "Every time I composed a poem, I wrote it down on a page from an account book, using a brush borrowed from the inn; then I threw the page into a battered basket. Altogether I traveled nine thousand miles (*li*). When I arrived at my villa at Hai-hsi on the twenty-sixth day of the twelfth month, I opened the basket and counted the lumps of paper. They totaled 315. So I had composed 315 poems."[1]

Written just two years before Kung's death, these quatrains not only represent the culmination of the poet's creativity but recapitulate the important undertakings and concerns of his life. Therefore, it is no accident that the biographical information provided in Chapter One draws heavily on this sequence; in fact, all but one of the poems quoted there have been taken from the Chi-hai quatrains. These quatrains present many of the poet's own statements on his intellectual viewpoints. To fully appreciate the

73

artistry of the Chi-hai quatrains, we should bear in mind that they
are the product of an imagination nourished by diverse philosophical and literary traditions, especially the ethical intent of Confucian
aesthetics and the Buddhist view of the ambiguous nature of both
language and the phenomenal world. These intellectual forces,
working in concert or at odds with one another, often add an underlying tension to the verbal harmony of the Chi-hai poems; the
result is a kind of "learned" poetry wherein a great deal of personal
experience and intellectual insight are compressed into a few lines.
Unlike the imagistic T'ang *chüeh-chü*, which at its best often
triumphs in a sudden fusion of scene and mood, Kung's Chi-hai
chüeh-chü generally excel in an adept use of discursive language and
a subtle appropriation of conventional idioms. For the purpose of
evaluating the skill with which Kung employs the *chüeh-chü* form,
some of the Chi-hai quatrains will be analyzed in the light of traditional critical criteria for the *chüeh-chü*. The discussion will
conclude with a comparison of these quatrains with Kung's earlier
poems examined in previous chapters.

I *Critical Criteria*

A *chüeh-chü* consists of four lines of equal length, with five or
seven characters to the line; it is a poem which hardly begins before
it ends. The paramount poetical consideration in the writing of
chüeh-chü must therefore be economy and suggestiveness. In the
opinion of Yang Tsai (1271–1323) of the Yüan dynasty, a *chüeh-chü*
should be trimmed to the utmost simplicity and yet remain haunting
in its reticence, so that "when a line ends, its meaning does not
end."[2] The Ming critic Wang Shih-chen (1526–90) analogizes the
composition of *chüeh-chü* to placing the multitudinous heavens into
a tiny room where they nevertheless retain all of their glistening
glory.[3] Liu Hsi-tsai (1813–81) of the Ch'ing dynasty likens the
appreciation of *chüeh-chü* to the recognition of a pole from its
shadow.[4] Similarly, Shen Te-ch'ien (1673–1769) comments on the
seven-character *chüeh-chü:* "Although its words are easy to understand, its sentiments are hard to fathom"; in other words, the
impact of a *chüeh-chü* goes beyond the first reading. The reader is
advised to dwell on a *chüeh-chü* until he gets the "music beyond the
strings, the flavor beyond the tasting."[5] Or, as Wang Yü-yang [6]
(1634–1711) put it, a good *chüeh-chü* shares with music the quality of "one plucking, three echoes" (*i-ch'ang san-t'an*).[7]

Another *chüeh-chü* guideline closely related to the brevity of its structure is the fluidity of thought and the coherence between consecutive lines. Unlike the eight-line *lü-shih* (or regulated verse), which must contain two pairs of parallel lines in the middle of the poem, a *chüeh-chü* does not have to observe the rule of parallelism. As a matter of fact, the consensus among critics is that it should not. Those *chüeh-chü* which lean heavily on parallelism have been considered unfinished *lü-shih*, or mockingly labeled "half of a *lü-shih*"; Tu Fu is a notable case.[8] The critical objection, however, is not leveled against parallelism itself but against the awkwardness and lack of movement which results from its strained use. If the parallel lines do flow smoothly from one to the other, then the parallelism does not mar the poem but instead may well make it noted for its ingenuity. The Ming critic Hu Ying-lin (1551–1602) cites two examples of successful parallelism in the *chüeh-chü*:[9] the first is a five-character *chüeh-chü* by Wang Chih-huan; the second is a seven-character *chüeh-chü* by Kao Shih, both famous poets of T'ang times.

Climbing the Heron Tower

(Chinese syntax) white sun across hills fades
Yellow River into sea flows
hoping exhaust thousand miles eye
further ascend one storey tower

(translation)   The bright sun fades across the hills.
The Yellow River flows into the sea.
Hoping to see all the sights,
I climb one more storey.

New Year's Eve

(Chinese syntax) travel house cold lamp alone not sleep
guest heart what reason turns sad-like
native land to-night think thousand miles
frosty temples to-morrow again one year

(translation)   By the cold lamp of an inn, alone and sleepless,
Why does this traveler's heart feel sad?
Tonight my native land beckons me from
    a thousand miles away;
Tomorrow my frosty temples will start to
    age another year.

Although both poems conclude with parallel lines, neither gives the impression of redundancy or duplication. The lines parallel each other syntactically but not semantically; the meaning of one line continues into the other in such a way that the thought in the latter line supplements that in the former. The parallelism, consequently, is hardly noticeable.

During the Ch'ing dynasty, Hu Ying-lin's opinions found strong support in the critical writings of Wang Fu-chih (1619–92). Like Hu, Wang refutes the idea that the *chüeh-chü* evolved structurally from the *lü-shih* as a result of permutation: that is, a *chüeh-chü* with two pairs of parallel lines can be traced back to the middle two parallel couplets of a *lü-shih;* a *chüeh-chü* which begins with a pair of parallel lines can be traced back to the second half of a *lü-shih;* and a *chüeh-chü* which concludes with a pair of parallel lines can be traced back to the first half of a *lü-shih.* In Wang's opinion, such theories merely destroy the poem's organic unity rather than explain its origin. He agrees with the contention that parallel lines in a *chüeh-chü* should flow smoothly from one to the other and cites the same example by Kao Shih to illustrate his point.[10] Wang's attitude toward parallelism and his high esteem for the seven-character *chüeh-chü* is evident from the following statement:

Whether or not a person has poetic talent and feeling can only be determined by attempting this genre. People who cannot handle the five-character Ancient Poem [*ku-shih*] are not worthy of belonging to the community of poets. People who cannot handle the seven-character *chüeh-chü* should simply stop writing poems. Merely searching for good parallel lines in the Contemporary Style is no more than sycophantic eulogizing with antithetic prose.[11]

Economy and fluidity are difficult enough to achieve in the writing of a *chüeh-chü;* there is, however, still a third requirement: the poet must effect change and variation in his work within the space of four lines. Ssu-k'ung T'u (837–908), a poet-critic of the T'ang dynasty, remarks that "The writing of *chüeh-chü* requires extreme artistry. Displaying a myriad of modes and a thousand variations, the *chüeh-chü* attains divine qualities without any trace of trying to be divine. How could this be easy?"[12] Chang Yen (1284–?) of the Sung dynasty observes that "The difficulty of writing short tunes for *tz'u* lyrics is equivalent to the difficulty of the *chüeh-chü* in the case of *shih* poems. . . . Not a single line or character can be superfluous."[13] The desire to make the best use of each of the four lines so that the quatrain may have beginning, development, change, and conclusion (traditionally referred to as the four steps of *ch'i, ch'eng, chuan,* and *ho*) constitutes another reason why parallelism is not advisable in the writing of *chüeh-chü.* In addition, critics often recommend that the third line receive special attention because it is in this line that the change of thought in the poem usually occurs. Yang Tsai, for example, summarizes the views of many when he says: "The skill of variation and change all depends on the third line. If the transition here is well effected, then the fourth line will follow like a boat gliding along with the current."[14] Shih Pu-hua (1835–90) of the Ch'ing dynasty elaborates upon a similar idea: "The intent of a seven-character *chüeh-chü* should reside in the third line. In that case, the fourth line has only to extend or elucidate it in order for the spirit and flavor of the poem to emerge automatically. If the intent of the poem lies in the fourth line, it is likely to end too abruptly. If the intent of the poem lies in the first and second lines, while both the third and fourth lines serve as mere extension and elucidation, then the poem will suffer from the lack of a crescendo. Therefore, the third line is the turning point. Although the former masters did not conform to this all the time, it is the best method."[15]

The fourth critical guideline for the *chüeh-chü* is the careful use of diction. As stated by Hu Ying-lin, somewhat impressionistically, "A five-character *chüeh-chü* aims at precision (*chen-ch'ieh*); therefore its subject matter usually overshadows its diction. A seven-character *chüeh-chü* aims at elegance (*kao-hua*); therefore its diction usually overshadows its subject matter."[16] Exemplary works of elegance can be found in the seven-character *chüeh-chü* of the High T'ang poet Wang Ch'ang-ling, also known as "the emperor of poets" (*shih t'ien-tzu*). Wang's style has been described as "exquisitely supple and gently florid" (*yu-jou wan-li*) by both Hu Ying-lin[17] and Shen Te-ch'ien,[18] and with Li Po he is regarded as the most skilled composer of the seven-character *chüeh-chü.* Perhaps it is not just a coincidence that by Late T'ang times, an epoch which stressed aesthetic refinement in poetry, writers of the seven-character *chüeh-chü* dominated the poetic scene while writers of the five-character *chüeh-chü* retreated to the background.[19] Although elegance is not the only preference of *chüeh-chü* masters, especially after the Late T'ang, it has remained a prominent objective of poets through the ages and serves as a convenient basis for the purposes of evaluation and comparison.

In the following pages an attempt will be made to elucidate the critical concepts outlined above by applying them to some of Kung Tzu-chen's Chi-hai quatrains. This is to place Kung's accomplishment in the *chüeh-chü* genre in the Chinese critical tradition, and to see how critical precepts and poetic examples can be brought into full performance in active reading. For the sake of clarity, each section will take up only one specific criterion and refract it through several poems. Some poems will be scrutinized under more than one criterion in order to arrive at a configurative pattern of understanding.

II *Economy and Suggestiveness*

A close look at Kung Tzu-chen's Chi-hai quatrains reveals two basic methods of attaining the twin ideals of economy and suggestiveness. The first is the conventional method of metaphorical presentation, whereby a word or trope is made to carry several orders of meaning simultaneously. The second method maximizes the poem's overall effect through deliberate reticence. The concomitant presence of both devices gives Kung's quatrains a consistent evocativeness.

Take, for example, the opening poem of this chapter. What at first glance seems like a curious juxtaposition of description and reflection is welded together by the metaphor of fallen petals. Starting with the first line, where the sunset provides a broad backdrop for the swelling sorrow of the traveler, Kung achieves an economy much like the illusion of depth in a painting: a distance of ten thousand miles is compressed into a foot of canvas. In line two, "the instant" is a translation of the character *chi* which, in this context, suggests not only distance but also great speed, and thus ushers in the critical fourth dimension—time. In line three, the focus shifts from distant views to foreground objects while direct description (line two) gives way to metaphor. The double negative "not without" emphasizes the unusual concept that petals can have feeling. More important than the personification of the petals, however, is the composite imagery of both lines: the reader receives the notion of a cycle which signifies continual attachment, renewal, and hope, and Kung manages this without any overt reference to these sentiments.

Another illustration of economy and suggestiveness by means of metaphor is No. 120 of these Chi-hai poems:

> Tight pegs, taut strings, I strum all alone;
> My tired eyes squint at the field overrun by weeds.
> The fragrant orchid concludes that it has effected
>   the wrong *karma*,
> Having been uprooted although it did not block
>   the road.   [K 521]

Unlike the previous poem which combines descriptive language with metaphorical observations, this quatrain is effected by a consistent metaphorical tone. "Tight pegs, taut strings" not only suggests a sense of mental fatigue which lays the ground for the concession to *karma* in the third line, but is also a possible reference to the poet's lofty but unappreciated ideas. The second line provides a correlative for the mood of despondency with a seemingly natural scene, the weed-choked field: this spatial image both links the state of mental gloom to that of desolation in nature and serves as the background for the "fragrant orchid," an obvious reference to the poet. The full implication of the conclusion cannot be understood without resorting to specific biographical facts. For our purpose, it suffices to point out that the mood of this poem contrasts markedly with that of the previous poem. Here Kung expresses his bitterness about being kept away from the court, the same court for which he felt such deep attachment when he left it. By speaking in metaphorical terms, he makes his point subtly.

Sometimes the message of a *chüeh-chü* is brought home by what is left unsaid. The following two poems, the first of which appeared earlier in Chapter One, are good examples of the power of reticence in the *chüeh-chü* medium.

Miscellaneous Poems of the Year Chi-hai [No. 6]

> I have also served at the Grand Secretariat with my books
>   and brushes.
> In a heavenly midnight breeze the jade bridle-bells kept me
>   company.
> I want to launder my spring robe, but refrain out of tender
>   regard
> For the traces of dewdrops from outside the Ch'ien-ch'ing
>   Gate.   [K 509]

Miscellaneous Poems of the Year Chi-hai [No. 252]

Having dissipated talents which could sway the nation,
I am content to serve a woman, to wait upon her liquid glances.
But fearing that her lover's heroic zeal might end,
She rolls up the screen as she tends her hair and gazes
    at the Yellow River.   [K 532]

The second line of No. 6 contains an allusion to Tu Fu: "Because of a breeze, I think of the jade bridle-bells" in the "Passing a Spring Night at the Censorate" *(Ch'un su tso-sheng)*, a poem which describes Tu's anxious waiting for the approach of dawn so that he can present a memorial to the throne. "Jade bridle-bells" alludes to the ancient custom of officials commuting to the hall of audience on horseback. Kung places himself in the same situation as Tu Fu, thus associating himself as well with the sense of loyalty and faithful service implied by the night-long vigil. Line three features a change from memories of the past to emotions of the present. By dwelling on his "tender regard" for even the slightest reminder of the imperial grounds, the poet effectively underlines his deep feeling for the dynasty. This is a case of "recognizing a pole by looking at its shadow," to use the analogy of Liu Hsi-tsai.

In No. 252, the overall effect comes from a compactness made possible by a series of contrasts: a boudoir scene versus the backdrop of implied grandeur; talents forceful enough to "sway the nation" versus the confinement of "liquid glances"; and the pathos of resignation ("I am content to serve a woman") versus the irony of tantalizing hope ("She rolls up the screen"). The tension increases with the appearance of the dramatic third person ("she") in the last two lines; the poet uses her to objectify his self-mocking attitude and consequently avoids the clumsiness of direct assertion. The lady's gaze toward the river is at once an admonition for his inertia and an encouragement to return to politics. Although the consequences of the pivotal verb "gazes" fall outside the scope of the poem, "the Yellow River," with its multifarious historic-political associations, points to the nation at large as well as to the past ambitions and future endeavors of the narrator. It is this interplay between the "I" and the "she," the trivial "wait upon" and the almost heroic "gazes at" which provides the quatrain with a significance beyond its surface meaning. The obvious impact of this kind of suggestiveness by implication may explain why critics have praised this poem as a superb example of *han-hsü*.[20]

III   *Fluidity and Coherence*

Commenting on the secrets of poetry writing, the modern poet-author Yü Ta-fu (1896–1945) singles out "separate phrases with interlocking ideas" *(tz'u-tuan i-lien)* as a key to success, and he credits Kung Tzu-chen with a unique mastery of this technique.[21] Yü's examples are all couplets from the Chi-hai quatrains. It is quite clear that by "separate phrases with interlocking ideas" he refers to the semantic interdependence between two consecutive lines. However, in putting his emphasis on the coherence of couplets rather than on the coherence of entire poems, Yü has failed to draw attention to the flexibility of the principle of semantic inter-relatedness. A large number of the Chi-hai quatrains show that even in the absence of syntactical links, the four lines in each poem can still achieve total cohesion through the resonance of ideas and the coordination of sounds and images. For the sake of illustration, this section will focus on examples which consist mostly of grammatically self-contained lines:

Miscellaneous Poems of the Year Chi-hai [No. 4]

This trip shall take me through hills to the east and north.
My image in the mirror looks passably young, still.
A white cloud floats along no fixed paths:
Alone it visits the world, alone it drifts away.   [K 509]

Miscellaneous Poems of the Year Chi-hai [No. 8]

The T'ai-hang range weaves steadily along;
Portentous, it crouches like a tiger west of the capital.
Sending me off as I snap my whip and head for the east,
These mountains stare silently at the heart of China.   [K 509]

Miscellaneous Poems of the Year Chi-hai [No. 10]

Few in history have taken or resigned an office with ease.
Suddenly I stop those centuries-old tears and leave Ch'ang-an.
I linger long over the criss-crossed ancient tracks,
Then turn as the Buddha turned from a mulberry tree
     after three nights.   [K 509]

No. 4, an orchestration of both sound and sense, revolves around the motif of journey and return. Besides the usual rhyme words at the end of the first, second, and fourth lines, and besides the usual

balance of complementary level and deflected tones in the whole
poem, internal rhymes occur in three of the four lines: *shan* with
shan in line one, *tung* in line one with *chung* and *hung* in line two,
and *chien* with *huan* in line four; and alliteration occurs in almost
one-third of the characters: *ch'ü, ching, ch'iang, chien, ching* (five
palatals); *chung, ch'u, ch'u* (three retroflexes). "Hills to the east and
north" literally reads "eastern hills and northern hills" in the
original.[22] The complementary repetitions of the word "hills" in line
one and of the word "alone" in the last line give the poem a kind of
symphonic structure. Thematically, the notion of an endless and
solitary journey suggested by lines one, three, and four receives an
ironic twist in line two, where, in spite of the poet's unwillingness to
accept it, the inexorable process of aging is underscored by the
subtle adverb "still." While sounds recur and echo one another in
the formal world of the poem, "white cloud" (that is, the natural
man) will eventually have to drift away.

In No. 8, visual effects supercede the structural impact. The four
lines unfold a majestic, dark-hued scene in which a woody area is
likened to the motley skin of a tiger. Both the poet on horseback and
the enveloping mountains seem to be moving; the poet snapping a
whip, the mountains meandering slowly onto the distant horizon.
"Capital" and "the heart of China" localize the setting and
superimpose an emotive tone on the word-picture. The poet's reluctance to leave the center of "portentous" actions is reflected in
the silent stare of the mountains.

No. 10 is a poem on a deceptively common theme. Here sounds
and images cease to be self-sufficient and are gathered into a net-
work of meanings through interacting allusions, ranging from the
personal-familial to the historical and religious. The presence of
history throughout the poem lifts the conventional theme of leave-
taking onto a higher plane. And history unfolds on two levels: the
imaginary and the actual. On the actual level, the poet-official resolves, after much hesitation, to resign a disappointing office. The
resolution is carried out, again with considerable agony, in the second half of the poem. Both his hesitation and his departure unfold
within the bounds of Confucian decorum, for a responsible scholar-
official is expected to relinquish a position in government with
reluctance. On the imaginary level, "centuries-old tears," "criss-
crossed ancient tracks," and the figurative capital Ch'ang-an (the
Ch'ing capital was in Peking, a much younger city) conjure up a
picture laden with historical associations. For example, the charac-

ter *ch'i* ("criss-crossed") has the double meaning of "variegation" and "chess," an apt association for Ch'ang-an: this city, the seat of government for many past dynasties, on the one hand was laid out in a regular grid pattern of streets and on the other hand was the arena of innumerable military victories and defeats.[23] The mulberry tree in the last line alludes to a Buddhist legend that the Buddha never stays under the same mulberry tree for more than three nights so that he will not become attached to any given place.[24] A footnote by the poet tells us that his family had occupied official positions in the capital for three generations. Such being the case, the allusion to the Buddhist legend becomes all the more pertinent. Lingering and turning away thus carry a particular personal note of sadness and serve to heighten the tension between the Confucian ideal of tradition and service and the Buddhist yearning for spiritual freedom. Hesitation ("linger") yields to resolution ("turn"), and resigning an office becomes a transcendental gesture—all within the compass of four lines.

Such total cohesion can be found even in quatrains containing parallel lines. Although only about a dozen of the 315 Chi-hai poems feature parallel lines, Kung Tzu-chen's treatment of this technical convention makes an interesting footnote to the observation of some critics that unobstrusive parallelism can enhance rather than obstruct the progress of thought in a poem. For example:

Miscellaneous Poems of the Year Chi-hai [No. 116]

A gifted man in middle age indulges in lurid music.
A hermit in lean years tires of rustic clothes.
Both sentiments are in fact excusable:
May the judgment of history be not too harsh.   [K 520]

Miscellaneous Poems of the Year Chi-hai [No. 28]

I cannot help but praise you to everyone:
So mad, so gallant, so gently refined.
Your heart shines on others like a Ch'in moon;
Your feelings at my departure resemble clouds above
    mountains.   [K 511]

Miscellaneous Poems of the Year Chi-hai [No. 147]

The prayer hall is fragrant with flowers rained from
    the sky;

> By the long river, we witness again the religious
>   essence.
> Let sparks of insight inspire the living verse:
> Lest mere words replace the magic of Zen.   [K 523]

Lines one and two of No. 116, besides being parallel in structure, also contain parallel experiences: a gifted man "indulges in lurid music" and a hermit "tires of rustic clothes"; in other words, neither remains true to the characteristics associated with his status—talent and asceticism respectively. We expect action of a gifted man and fortitude of a lofty recluse; instead we are shown the hermit on the verge of renouncing his vow of simplicity because of the pressure of hard times and the gifted man in frantic pursuit of sensual pleasure because he has already passed his prime. The two lines thus refer to the same kind of experience: idealism gone sour in the face of reality. Line one, indeed, is evidently an apology by Kung for his weak indulgences. Line two reinforces the reason for the collapse of will implied in the first line and is consequently essential to the plea for understanding which follows in lines three and four.

The second poem involves a double parallelism, one structural and one concealed. The poet's affection for his friend and the friend's reciprocal feelings on the occasion of the poet's departure provide the basis for mutual identification throughout the poem. What is said about the "you" is equally applicable to the "I." Once this is granted, the admirable qualities ascribed to the surrogate "I" begin to take on biographical relevance, and the textual parallelism in lines three and four progresses logically from the first two lines. "Heart" here is a translation of the Chinese term *tan* (literally "gall"), which has the connotation of openness and courage and therefore echoes the adjectives "mad" *(k'uang)* and "gallant" *(hsia)* in line two. "Feelings" in line four is a far from perfect translation of the word *ch'ing*, which encompasses a whole range of positive human traits such as gentility and refinement *(wen-wen)* ascribed to the I/You earlier. The brightness and impartiality suggested by "Ch'in moon" and the lingering sentiment mirrored in "clouds above mountains" can only come from a person who, like the poet himself, has witnessed many parting scenes and is well aware of the vicissitudes of life.

The third exemplary poem was written specifically for a lecturer of Buddhist scriptures who had the distinction of having financed the reprinting of one of the Sutra texts. The whole poem revolves around the paradox of ritual and faith, language and intuitive understanding. "Flowers rained from the sky" in line one alludes to the legend of a Buddhist monk in the Six Dynasties. His sermon was allegedly so moving that flowers rained down from heaven. "The long river," which refers to the Yangtze, is the place where this miracle was supposed to have occurred.[25] "Inspire the living verse" (*ts'an huo-chü*) brings to mind Wang Yü-yang's laudatory remark on the inimitable excellence of Wang Wei, a T'ang poet well known for the Zen flavor in his quiet lines.[26] The allusion to Zen and the place of Zen in poetry becomes explicit in line four, which, besides accentuating the central paradox of the poem, also sums up the poet's lifelong attitude toward literary pursuits: words, however perfectly ordered, represent nothing more than substitute experience and are not to be mistaken for the ultimate reality which can only be appropriated through transcendental insights. Here the irony runs deep: the poet employs two well-wrought parallel lines to refute the validity of words, and thereby propels the poem onto a different plane of meaning.

IV   *Variation and Change*

For a poetic form in which everything must be said within four lines, Chang Yen's observation that "not a single line or character can be superfluous" is literally true. In fact, a great deal of the critical controversy over the place of parallelism in the *chüeh-chü* form is directly related to the problem of the best way to distribute the semantic weight within a quatrain. Some critics think it absolutely necessary that the poet effect a turn of thought or a shift of mood or scene in mid-poem, preferably in the third line, so to prevent a *chüeh-chü* from becoming fragmentary or static. This change, however, must be smooth and organically related to the preceding lines. Consequently, some kind of transition is needed. Let us now examine Kung Tzu-chen's *chüeh-chü* and see how this principle of change, or *pien-hua*, operates in specific contexts.

There are basically two kinds of transition which effect a change in Kung's *chüeh-chü*. For the sake of convenience, we shall label them the *explicit* type and the *implicit* type. The explicit type of transition generally coincides with some grammatical sign, whereas the implicit type, as evidenced in the opening poem of this chapter, is so well integrated into the texture of the poem that only a close reading will reveal its true nature. Both types of transition can be effective, depending upon how they fit into the tone and conceptual scheme of the poem. First, the explicit type:

Miscellaneous Poems of the Year Chi-hai [No. 107]

In my youth, upon assuming office, I aimed at pacifying the world;
I am tired now—pity this hour of retirement!
But today I no longer shed my idle tears;
In crossing the river, I miss only her charming presence.   [K 519]

Miscellaneous Poems of the Year Chi-hai   [No. 255]

The *feng* roams, the *luan* wanders, each with its own sorrow.*
For three lives I have dreamed of Soochow, florid and foliant.
The sunset by my childhood home no longer seems the same;
I envy the boat-woman who has never left Tiger Hill.   [K 533]

*The *feng* is the male and the *luan* the female of the fabled "phoenix."

Miscellaneous Poems of the Year Chi-hai [No. 315]

As the verses stop, all nature seems opaque.
So many things have yet to be said in the lamp's low light.
Suddenly, without a word, I put down my brush
And turn again to the seven volumes of the *Lotus Sutra*.   [K 538]

These three poems share two things in common: (1) there is a change of mood, of temporal framework, or of spatial relationship in the third line; and (2) the change is signaled by certain time-space indicators. In No. 107, the word "today" underscores the poet's current state of fatigue and weariness which makes the "crossing" all the more poignant, since in the past he was active and ambitious. In No. 255, the phrase "my childhood home" both links the specific locale of Tiger Hill, a scenic spot in Soochow, with the flowery metropolis, Soochow, and at the same time contrasts the regional stability and the mindless simplicity of the boat-woman with the agonizing drifting of the poet. "Three lives" has a strong Buddhist flavor, as has been pointed out in a previous chapter. No. 315 is an intriguing example of how a personal philosophy can serve as the agent of *pien-hua*.

At the outset of the third line in this poem (No. 315), "suddenly"—one of Kung's favorite expressions—signals a change of narrative direction and prepares the reader for some emotional relief from the "opaque" environment of the first two lines. This relief however, does not materialize as expected. The awaited emotional break turns out to be further silence. With "so many things" yet to be captured in language, the poet suddenly stops writing and returns instead to the hushed world of religious contemplation. This poem, the last of the Chi-hai cycle, reaffirms the power of transcendental wisdom over the "things" in nature and the "words" which are supposed to represent the reality of things. The distrust of language here is characteristic of Kung. In the very first line of the first Chi-hai poem, he asks: "How can writing a book be compared with observing the mind?" Paradoxically enough, the suddenness conveyed by the word "suddenly" is not that sudden after all.

The implicit type of transition is more difficult to pinpoint. It usually takes the form of a change in subject matter, a shift in visual perspective, or a leap in thematic scope. For instance, in the opening poem of this chapter, the third line, "Petals fall but not without feeling," does not, on the surface, bear any logical relationship with the first half of the poem, which is a general description of the poet's feelings of forlornness at parting. To appreciate the organic unity of the two halves of the poem, we must associate the poet's reluctant leave-taking with the natural incidence of petals falling deciduously. Once this connection is perceived, the impact of the last line becomes clear: the painful parting is not final; just as the fallen petals will become the seed bed for the next spring and "nurture flowers again," the poet will be reunited in spirit with the party he leaves behind. It is this fusion of public language and private experience which makes this poem unique.

Sometimes the change occurs when the poet shifts his visual perspective, like the use of different camera angles. A notable example of this is No. 252, discussed earlier under economy and suggestiveness. In the first two lines, the narrator makes an aside: "Having dissipated talents which could sway the nation,/I am content to serve a woman, to wait upon her liquid glances." But then the "camera" switches to the woman who "rolls up the screen . . . and gazes at the Yellow River." Her motive in calling her lover's attention to the outside world ("fearing that her lover's heroic zeal might end") associates the man's resigned servitude to love and the woman's high-minded concern for the man. Accompanying this visual double-exposure is also a change of voice; the last two lines are third-person. Without the double change—point of view and voice—the poem would lose a great deal of its dramatic impact.

Thematic mutation is still a third way by which a transition is implicitly effected in a *chüeh-chü*. In the following quatrain, the two halves of the poem, one scene-centered and the other reflective, are unified by a common motif:

Miscellaneous Poems of the Year Chi-hai [No. 225]

Silver candle; autumnal hall; I listen alone . . . .
Who reports a heavy rain outside the screen?
Tomorrow no one can admire the scene along the creek,
For the creek bridge will be flooded over, a foot deep. [K 530]

The main motif of this *chüeh-chü* concerns rain and its aftermath. In the first half of the poem, the rain remains in the background; it is reported to the narrator in an atmosphere of frail candlelight and a shadowy hall, an atmosphere hauntingly familiar in classical Chinese poetry. The poet has thus prepared us for additional inward response to the scene, possibly a soft-edged picture of another autumn or fleeting faces. But, on the contrary, the poetic voice assumes a matter-of-fact tone in the third and concluding lines. It expresses a quiet concern for what the all-night storm will do to the landscape "outside the screen." Now the scene evoked by the first two lines fades into the background. After the heavy rain, says the poet, the creek bridge will be submerged under water, and there will be no way for the prospective tourist to see the beauty of the hills. A sense of regret over the imagined disappearance of the bridge pervades the concluding lines: the idea of a lost scene, a lost chance, predominates the entire poem. Thus we see that in the first two lines the poet has planted the seed of the crucial idea of "chance missing." The image of rain serves to bridge together a concrete experience and an anxiety which is universal and not as rain-bound.

V *Multifaceted Language*

So far we have examined Kung Tzu-chen's *chüeh-chü* mainly from a structural point of view, guided and inevitably restricted at each turn by the special nomenclature of traditional Chinese critical terminology. It is now time to take up the fourth and last critical guideline and examine the Chi-hai quatrains from a different perspective: that of language.

The diction of Kung's *chüeh-chü* is wide-ranging and, on the whole, combines a subtle blend of conventional idiom and personal symbolism. On the conventional side, he draws freely from a variety of sources, ranging from archaic terms from the pre-Han classics to colloquial expressions of the folk ballad. In so doing, he speaks as a public poet utilizing a medium which is to a greater or lesser extent easily understood. Falling within the range of this public language are: (1) well-known literary allusions, often invested with allegorical significance; (2) historical references used as a narrative shorthand; and (3) religious terms, mostly Buddhist, appropriated for philosophical purposes.

An obvious example of Kung's use of literary allusions is the "fragrant orchid" in line three of No. 120 (p. 79), in which there is a tacit analogy between the orchid and the narrator. Here the poet presupposes the reader's familiarity with the word-image *lan* (orchid), which has connoted "virtuous beauty" as early as Ch'ü Yüan's "Encountering Sorrow" (*Li sao*), a long autobiographical poem dating from the fourth century B.C. Therefore, in lamenting the orchid's fate of unprovoked uprooting, the poet is actually utilizing a public symbol to convey a private mood.

This principle of achieving narrative economy through a shared common knowledge between the poet and the reader also operates in lines involving historical and religious references. Unlike the literary allusions of the *lan* (orchid) type which compress the tenor and the vehicle into one term, historical allusions are usually used to build a narrative structure that underlies the surface simplicity of the quatrain. For example, "judgment of history" in line four of No. 116 (p. 83) is only a paraphrase of the original *yang-ch'iu pien-pi*, which alludes to the historical belief that in the *Spring and Autumn Annals*, a chronicle of major events in the feudal states from 721 to 481 B.C., Confucius reveals his moral position on the actions of the ruling elite through a careful choice of words in recording these events. His approval or condemnation of a moral or political act supposedly resides in the language used in the narrative. And such an evaluative approach to history has ever since been one of the features of Chinese historiography. Hence, in a phrase like *yang-ch'iu pien-pi* a whole tradition of Chinese historical writing is

summed up in a few words. There are other allusions of a more
learned nature which we shall not go into here. It suffices to say
that, in combing through history for analogical experiences, Kung
the poet is speaking in unison with Kung the scholar, whose absorption in history and state affairs makes him a link in the long
chain of statesman-scholar-poets.

Besides literary and historical allusions, religious terms also appear in the Chi-hai poems, especially in those which depict the
poet's quieter, reflective moods. Most of these terms are Buddhist
in origin; their conceptual referents have already, through popular
usage, become the bedrock of the Chinese philosophical outlook on
life. Thus in using such familiar terms as *san-sheng* (three lives),
ch'ien-yin (*karma*), and *k'ung-sang* (illusory mulberry tree), the poet
reveals not only the lyrical side of his erudite mind but also a collective religious consciousness which is shared by all strata of society, the elite as well as the common people.

Such multiple and synthetic borrowings from the repertory of
public language, coupled with a preponderant interest in ideas,
sometimes give Kung's *chüeh-chü* diction a discursive quality which
contrasts markedly with the lean, imagistic lines of T'ang poetry.
However, even in handling the conventional side of his language,
Kung Tzu-chen commands a spectrum of styles:

Miscellaneous Poems of the Year Chi-hai [No. 16]

A banished wife urges her little sister-in-law:
"Take care of mother who has been so good to us."
She rattles on about necessities, starting with
    rice and salt;
Though tears soak her red skirt, she cannot bear to go. [K 510]

Miscellaneous Poems of the Year Chi-hai [No. 117]

The ancient clothes of the Chi and Chiang clans are
    no longer worn.[27]
Like the Chao women, ladies nowadays step daintily
    in sharp-pointed slippers.[28]
But when a lord seeks a consort worthy of an ancestral
    temple,
Should virtue's reputation[29] depend on delicate toes?   [K 520]

In diction and style, no two *chüeh-chü* poems can be farther apart than these. The first piece is conversational in tone and is couched in the plain, unadorned language of the folk ballad. Not only are the personae *ch'i fu* (banished wife) and *hsiao ku* (little sister-in-law) familiar figures in the *yüeh-fu* poems (popular or art ballads) of earlier times, but the atmosphere of subdued sorrow at parting is even reminiscent of some early prototypes, such as the long ballad "Chiao Chung-ch'ing's Wife." Apart from a deliberate use of colloquial language ("She rattles on about . . . rice and salt"), Kung here has also borrowed one of the time-honored ballad themes—the wronged wife/daughter-in-law and the pathos of her concerns at the moment of departure—to dramatize his own undying affection for the Ch'ing court, however foolhardy and indiscriminate it might be.[30]

The second poem, on the other hand, employs a language which stands at the other extreme of conventional diction. Topical in nature and satiric in tone, the poem attacks the custom of foot binding in a highly allusive language which proves almost baffling upon first reading. Terms and phrases culled from the *Shih ching* and the *Shih chi* (see n. 27–29) are summoned to body forth a corrective social message: foot binding, which has victimized too many Chinese women for too long, not only is an unnatural practice but runs counter to cultural tradition as well. The ancients were sensible enough to prefer physical comfort to dainty "pointed slippers." Virtue is a characteristic that does not depend upon the condition of one's toes. The language of the poem also harks back across the centuries to the sonorous ancestral hymns of the Chou people collected in the *Shih ching*, or *Book of Songs*, the first anthology of Chinese poetry, datable to the tenth century B.C. *Hui yin* (virtue's reputation) in line four is a term in praise of King Wen's consort in the *Shih ching* context and seems to have been chosen deliberately by Kung to give moral weight to his social criticism. The Manchus, for instance, do not subscribe to foot binding; and they are the ruling people, just like the Chou aristocrats commemorated in the ancient odes. Here the medium embodies the message.

Neither colloquialism nor scholarly erudition, however, represents Kung Tzu-chen's *chüeh-chü* language at its most endearing and memorable. Apart from reliance on literary convention and public sources, there is another side to Kung's diction which has earned him the reputation of an accomplished poet in the lyric mode: when he doffs the cloak of a scholar or a social critic and speaks with the voice of a private person, he speaks a unique and resilient language, a language often charged with deep-felt emotions.

The uniqueness of Kung Tzu-chen's use of language, whether in the *chüeh-chü* or other forms, comes from his ability to inspire old, threadbare word-images with fresh meanings. Putting new wine into old bottles has always been the task of poets who conform to conventional literary styles. A nineteenth-century poet writing at the close of a long literary tradition, Kung Tzu-chen is no exception. In order to be linguistically innovative and at the same time honor formal regulations, he pilfers stock images from the common hoard of literary diction and turns them into carriers of private moods and experience. In this he succeeds too well, so much so that he can be said to have created a private symbolism of his own, a rare feat in classical Chinese poetry. As we have noted earlier, two central images—*hsiao* (flute) and *chien* (sword)—played an integrating role in his poetry throughout his long writing career. These two images, both rather hackneyed in classical Chinese poetry, are consistently and lyrically used in shifting contexts, including some of the Chi-hai poems which we shall take up in the concluding section of this chapter. As private symbols, *hsiao* and *chien* stand for two ideal aspects of human endeavor and of the whole personality: aesthetic pursuits and heroic action. How to accommodate these two poles of attraction within one career was the central concern of the poet, both in life and in poetry. The concomitance of the flute and the sword creates a recurrent tension in his verse. A third unifying image, *lo-hung* (fallen petals), recurs significantly in the Chi-hai series, the poet's last creative output before his death. From the ideal man, suggested by the twin images of flute and sword, to the fallen man, mirrored in the metaphor of withering petals, the poet traveled a long way. It was a long journey of feeling, a persistent search for the right words by which feelings can be captured in language.

Another source of lyrical power comes from the sensual and associative quality of certain image-clusters, images which are frequently interwoven in a fluid syntax:

(Chinese syntax)

feng	p'o	luan	p'iao	pieh	yu	ch'ou
feng	roam	*luan*	wander	each	has	sorrow

san-sheng	hua-ts'ao	meng	Su-chou
three lives	flower-grass	dream	Soochow

(Translation)

> The *feng* roams, the *luan* wanders, each with its
>   own sorrow.
> For three lives [I] have dreamed of Soochow, florid
>   and foliant.
>   —from No. 255, translated on p. 86

In these lines there is a prevailing atmosphere of dreamy haziness brought out by word-pictures superimposed upon one another, almost like a montage. The modulating movement of the birds' roaming punctuates a long dreaming process which began in the dim past and flows into the future. But who is doing the dreaming? Collective humanity? The sentient vegetative life? Or is it the eternal poet? The syntax of the second line does not define the direction for the reader's response, and it seems to be the poet's intention not to define it. He chooses to let the floating images speak for themselves or enter into free relationships with one another without the burden of prose grammar. It is this kind of ornate diction and fluid syntax that traditional critics have in mind when they use the term *kao-hua* (elegance) to characterize the typical language of seven-character *chüeh-chü*.

Finally, at its most disarming, this personal language is capable of being both general and specific; it can bracket off a few particular moments from the flow of time:

> Miscellaneous Poems of the Year Chi-hai [No. 207]
>   —In remembrance of the lilacs

> Years ago, upon turning twenty, I sought fragrant blooms;
> Their charm glittered like exquisite gems.
> It has been hard to forget the red clay monastery
>   in the fine rain;
> There I leaned against this flower on that spring day,
>   my fur coat soaking wet.   [K 529]

"Fragrant blooms" and a quiet monastery in a fine rain—these are the ostensible objects of the poet's remembrance. But notice the difference in language in the two halves of the poem. The first two lines feature a language which is general and imprecise, as if chosen to further adumbrate a fading memory. In the Chinese original, the "fragrant blooms," figuratively the objects of the poet's amorous adventures, are compared to *ling-lung wan-yü* literally "crystalline ten-thousand jades," a very conventional descriptive phrase used to suggest either bejeweled women or simply the idea of wealth and elegance. The only point of interest here is the time indicator. The poet had reached manhood and was ready for new experiences. By the third line the objects of remembrance begin to assume a soft contour with the introduction of the red-clayed monastery and spring rain; moreover, the language becomes progressively less general. Finally, in the concluding line the remembered scene comes into sharp focus in words like *i* (leaning) and *tz'u hua* (this flower). The poet does not after all remember the lilacs so much as he remembers the erstwhile youth who leaned against the blooming lilacs, seeking experience of all forms—in this case, romantic adventure.

Before we conclude, it may be of some relevance to reflect that, of all the compositional and evaluative principles enumerated by the traditional critics, the one pertaining to diction is probably the most impressionistic. The dichotomy between *chen-ch'ieh* (precision) and *kao-hua* (elegance) (proposed by Hu Ying-lin) is more apparent than real. In good hands, the language of a seven-character *chüeh-chü* can be both elegant and precise.

VI *Exile and Homecoming*

In focusing upon the internal properties of the Chi-hai quatrains, we have treated these poems primarily as a group of exemplary pieces in the *chüeh-chü* genre, almost as a separate entity in Kung Tzu-chen's long creative career. We shall now remove this artificial boundary between poet and poetry and place the Chi-hai poems in a larger and more existential context. After all, these quatrians, 315 in all, were written toward the close of the poet's life; they were composed impromptu during a leisurely "homeward" trip which lasted altogether eight months. They are, therefore, the final records not only of the culminating phase of a fertile and active mind but also of a life in transit, physically and emotionally. In order to see the last phase of Kung Tzu-chen's life, particularly the complexity of his inward struggle, we must follow his journey, which the Chi-hai quatrains chronicle from the very beginning.

On the twenty-third day of the fourth month of the year Chi-hai

(1839), Kung Tzu-chen, whose heart for three decades had been equally divided between serving the sword and tending the flute, forswore the former by withdrawing from officialdom for a life of "observing the mind" (*kuan hsin;* Chi-hai Poems, Nos. 1 and 2). On that late spring day, he left the capital once and for all. He had proffered gratuitously to the court his scathing and far-reaching insights into the state of the nation, but largely to no avail. The Ch'ing court was too paralyzed by inertia and conservatism to heed the pleas, no matter how urgent, of one "minor official." He had tried his hand at a variety of scholarly pursuits and earned for himself more than a modest share of recognition among literary circles. But literary success without the concomitant action of the sword was at best only a mocking one, a success by default. In the spring of the year Chi-hai, Kung was approaching forty-eight, well into the twilight years of life by traditional account, and still trapped in a lackluster career. A thoroughly disappointed man, he began to look homeward to the lush greenery of the south and to a sheltered old age of Zen contemplation. Only a short while earlier he had vowed for the third time in his reluctant creative life not to wallow in the mire of language any longer; yet to express his feelings upon his withdrawal from public life, Kung repented and made a final surrender to the flute. The result was 315 poems.

Such is the biographical background of the Chi-hai quatrains. Compared with the poet's earlier writings, this last group of poems is considerably quieter in tone and more restrained in language. We no longer find in them the sardonic humor permeating the earlier fables, the exuberant and hyperbolic language of the rolling ancient songs *(ko-hsing)* or the playful use of arcane terms characteristic of the poet's "strange" compositions (see Chapter Three). In their stead, there is a set of new and unifying images such as "fallen petal" and "twilight time" *(ch'ih-mu* or *ch'ui-mu),* suggestive of a frame of mind bordering on total resignation. In these extemporaneous *chüeh-chü* lines, the aging poet records in sparse words both some of the intense moments in his past and several wishes for a less stormy future.

The Kung Tzu-chen who emerges from these Chi-hai quatrains is a man of multiple concerns and changing moods. A careful reading of the poems written at the outset of the leisurely homeward trek, when the poet was still in the vicinity of the capital, bears out the multiplicity of conflicts in his heart. In the first two poems his mood is one of tranquility *(p'ing-tan)*, since he has decided to wave farewell to the kaleidoscopic life of the capital and looks forward to an eventless retirement, untainted by either political ambitions or the enticement of women. Yet in the very next poem he is engrossed in his concern over the fate of the court, which he depicts as besieged by predatory beasts; in addition, he mentions his gratitude for the magnanimous patronage of the dragon-throne:

Miscellaneous Poems of the Year Chi-hai [No. 3]

A fierce, evil wind shakes the soul of spring.
Tigers and leopards crouch gloomily at the nine gates
     of Heaven.[31]
Yet the fallen flower remains calm and cheerful,
Always cherishing in silence the Jade Emperor's favor.   [K 509]

Kung's departure, therefore, is not as nonchalant an act as it may sound. His decision to leave involved heart-rending choices and a final severance of political and emotional ties formed of three generations' loyal service to the court. His inward struggle is superbly dramatized in No. 10 (discussed in section III): the poet lingers over many an ancient track in the capital and finally pulls himself away like the Buddha's turning away from the illusory mulberry tree. And throughout the Chi-hai cycle Kung is ever concerned about the state of the nation and the welfare of the common people (see Nos. 123, 21, 83, and 297, translated on pp. 23 and 49–50). For example, in the following prayer written for a Taoist temple, he says:

Miscellaneous Poems of the Year Chi-hai [No. 125]

Life forces of the empire depend on wind and thunder.
Ten thousand muted horses are a sad sight indeed.
I urge old heaven to perk up again
And send down talent, unlimited in kind.   [K 521]

If Kung's break with his public past is more apparent than real, his plans for a private life in the future also recall the philosophy of his younger days. Time and again his mood wavers between romantic abandonment and religious idealism:

Miscellaneous Poems of the Year Chi-hai [No. 276]

In my youth I belittled the founders of Shang and Chou,
But not Shih-huang and Wu-ti of Ch'in and Han.
Imagine a hero in his declining years:
Where can he dwell but in the land of love? [K 534]

Miscellaneous Poems of the Year Chi-hai [No. 278]

After many ordeals the flower from heaven perceives
 its incarnation;
Who to distract me from meditation is also predestined.
By a lone lamp in an ancient inn I sit pure-hearted,
Different from the one you dream of, beside the pearly
 screen. [K 534]

Miscellaneous Poems of the Year Chi-hai [No. 275]

Luckily, my unique writings worthy of monasteries[32]
 were completed early.
What other way is there to spend this life?
From now on, after burning the incense and paying respect
 to Buddha,
I shall focus my attention on you, as predestined. [K 534]

Three different attitudes toward old age and love are involved
here. In the first poem, the rhetorical question of the concluding
line implies a kind of hedonism fraught with anxiety and mental
anguish. The two historical personages mentioned in line two were
both men of titanic ambitions—men who, because of their intemperate personalities, have earned a dubious reputation in history.
By singling out these two emperors for admiration, the poet reveals
his partiality for unorthodox historical heroes. In the second poem,
love is considered to be a distraction from spiritual pursuits, not a
solution to loneliness; retirement should be a time during which one
cultivates one's inner self through meditation and abstemiousness.
These two antipoles, human affection and religious detachment, are
then united in the third poem: here, love and the worship of
Buddha are treated on the same transcendental plane as two ways of
achieving tranquility and enlightenment.
 Kung's fondness for juxtaposing religious and romantic elements,
like the "abandoned madness," or *k'uang*, reflected in his partiality

for unorthodox personages, of course reminds us of the poet in his youth. The difference is in his sadder tone. The flowers which used to symbolize romantic adventures have now either turned into fallen petals or become objects of remembrance; for instance:

Miscellaneous Poems of the Year Chi-hai [No. 247]

Spoken from atop the crane on a heavenly breeze,[33]
    a mere word
Can revive the souls of flowers fallen since time
    immemorial.
My traveling garb is not stained by ordinary tears;
They spring from a lifetime of unreturned favors.   [K 532]

Miscellaneous Poems of the Year Chi-hai [No. 245]

Fragrant and fragile as a cardamon flower when she
    first spoke—
Words which break the heart in recollection.
How can the peony of rare beauty, basking in spring warmth,
Ever be the plum blossom, mate of the recluse?[34]   [K 532]

We do not know the identity of the person "atop the crane" (presumably someone from a noble family) or of "the peony of rare beauty" (presumably a sing-song girl), but the "flowers fallen" and the "recluse" clearly refer to the poet himself. Both poems commemorate a romance which came to naught. The mournful tone and the bitter-sweet language typify many Chi-hai quatrains; some of them read like swan songs at the end of a lonely yet spectacular journey:

Miscellaneous Poems of the Year Chi-hai [No. 36]

Drawn by your refinement, I often bare my heart.
Literary ties are as stong as blood ties.
Today I have a few tearful words over a cup of wine:
A hero in declining years sees the value of gold.[35]   [K 512]

Miscellaneous Poems of the Year Chi-hai [No. 96]

In my youth I wielded the sword and played the flute.
But gone are my sword-like valor and flute-like heart;

> Who could have foreseen this desolation upon my
>   returning home,
> When a myriad of joys and sorrows converge upon me?   [K 518]

The squanderer of bygone days has come to realize the importance of gold and the true worth of human ties. The poet-official finally sees the evanescent nature of both the flute and the sword. Perhaps Kung can best achieve equanimity in the company of a kindred spirit or a tender soul, for the private and introverted side of him ultimately shuns even the quiet world of literary associations for dreams, fantasies, and intimate reminiscences. This side of Kung is most evident in his *tz'u* lyrics, which we shall examine in the next chapter.

CHAPTER 5

Lake Clouds and Dreams:
Kung Tzu-chen as a Tz'u Poet

> Mine is not undue grieving or groundless sorrow,
> But turning into verse what I have seen and felt.
> Perhaps these hundred thousand pearly words
> Will buy the hearts of lovers for ages to come.
> —"Written at the End of the *Lyrics from the Studio of Red Dhyāna*"[1] [No. 3, K 470]

THESE half-apologetic and half-wishful lines capsulize what Kung Tzu-chen thinks of his *tz'u* poetry, a lyric form he favored at both ends of his creative life. He started to compose *tz'u* at the age of nineteen, printed four collections at thirty-two, and completed a remarkable literary career with a fifth *tz'u* collection in 1840, a year before he died.[2] He was, therefore, from beginning to end a *tz'u* poet. Yet despite his persistent interest, Kung was never entirely at home with the genre and was often compelled to justify his *tz'u* works;[3] his efforts at justification reflect a love-rejection anxiety which besets many *tz'u* practitioners, an anxiety whose cause must be sought in literary history.

The *tz'u* originated in Late T'ang times as verses specifically composed or adapted to fit musical tunes.[4] The requirements of music impose two formal features on the *tz'u*: its lines tend to be irregular in length to conform to the particular musical scores; and the lines, being frequently fragmented, tend to cohere in clusters to round off a thought process. Both formal features are a considerable departure from the conventional *shih*, which is characterized by even line length and line- or couplet-centered syntax. As time went by, what began as innovations gradually crystallized into literary conventions, and poets began to compose *tz'u* lyrics according to prosodic patterns prescribed by old tune titles, although many of the musical scores had begun to disappear in the Southern Sung period. By Ch'ing times, the separation of music and *tz'u* was complete and irrevocable; the *tz'u* had entered a new stage of maturity as a self-contained literary form.

The divorcement of music and *tz'u*, however, did not totally free the latter of its dubious status as a hybrid form, an adopted child to both music and *shih*. The *tz'u* emerged after the *shih* and was treated from its inception as a derivative form. And unlike the *shih*, which is wide-ranged in diction and subject matter, the *tz'u*, initially written as song lyrics, features a language and style which are predominantly delicate and lilting, often "precious." Consequently, the narrative scope of the *tz'u* is often confined to that of languid moods, intangible sorrows, or unabashed lovesickness, accompanied by typical settings such as the incense-filled atmosphere of a boudoir, the gilded interior of a palace, or a soft-colored landscape. Although at times the *tz'u*, with its resilient syntax and supple rhythm, eclipsed the *shih* and proved to be a better medium for the delineation of overflowing feelings, high-minded poet-literati of the past have by and large held the genre suspect and considered its composition a pastime rather than a calling.[5] Critics too chose to label this form *shih-yü*, a term which may mean both "a derivation of *shih*" and "an extension of *shih*"; thus just as the *tz'u* poets felt uncertain about their genre in practice, so too did its critics in theory.[6]

Kung Tzu-chen's reservations about the *tz'u* as a poetic medium sprang primarily from a personal skepticism of the purpose and potency of expressive language, and were only tangentially related to the orthodox view of decorum and propriety. In fact, in his defense of his *tz'u* compositions in the "Self-Preface to my Irregular Verses" (*Ch'ang-tuan-yen tzu-hsü*), he countered the moralistic view by emphasizing the necessity of giving strong emotion (*ch'ing*) spontaneous exposure in measured sounds, the quintessence of *tz'u* poetry:

Emotion, this thing, I once had the good mind of extirpating. Yet try as I did, I ended up condoning it. And what was mere condoning at the start eventually grew to be an attitude of reverence. Why after all did Master

Kung compose his *tz'u* verses if not for the revering of emotion? And of emotions and feelings, the most venerable are those which are not abiding, those which have no specific referents, those which suggest both reality and unreality, those which point out by not pointing, and those which, though caused by joy and sorrow, are not bound by joy and sorrow. Wherein do these emotions manifest themselves? They are manifested in sounds . . . [K 232]

A similar vein of thinking underlies the poem quoted above. In stating that his *tz'u* lyrics are in essence genuine experiences recast in words, Kung tacitly refutes the orthodox prejudice against the *tz'u* as an impure form which feeds on affected sentiments and trivial emotions. By boldly defining the prospective audience of his *tz'u* as the tender-hearted eternal "lovers," he extends to the genre a candid acceptance long overdue. In the following pages we shall examine some of Kung's *tz'u* from the perspective of thematic unity and see how they correlate with his creative precept that the highest order of *ch'ing* (emotions, feelings, the positive desires of a sentient being) constitutes a reality which points to, but is in substance independent of, the world of fixed referents. A few words will be said toward the end of this chapter about Kung Tzu-chen's place in the context of Ch'ing *tz'u* as a whole.

I *Dreamland*

The first four collections of Kung's *tz'u*, selected and edited over a period of two years, came out in 1823: *Unfettered Lyrics (Wu-cho tz'u-hsüan); Lyrics from the Hall of Remembrance (Huai-jen-kuan tz'u-hsüan); Lyrics of Allusion (Ying-shih tz'u-hsüan);* and *Lyrics of Minor Tranquility (Hsiao she-mo [śamatha] tz'u-hsüan).*[7] The Buddhist slant in the choice of titles was obviously intentional; and the *Unfettered Lyrics* was originally entitled *Lyrics from the Studio of Red Dhyāna (Hung-ch'an-shih tz'u).*[8] Concealed in these allusive terms is an ubiquitous metaphor that all forms of heightened consciousness—the untiring upward drive of the spirit, the fanciful play of the creative imagination, the relentless workings of memory, or the meditative activities of the mind—partake of the essence and intensity of a dream; and the moment of awakening, the moment of cognitive reflection, is also the moment of irremediable loss and tragic descent. The life-dream analogy is of course no novelty in Chinese literature, but rarely has the dream metaphor been treated with such fervid concentration in poetry.

The dream motif develops in Kung Tzu-chen's *tz'u* in many ways and on different planes. It can be explicit, as in the case of many "dream songs" in the *Unfettered Lyrics,* where dreaming becomes actual experience replete with vivid details about environs and personae, sometimes accompanied by authorial notes explaining the circumstances under which the dream took place. Or it can be implicit, when the line between descriptive reality and creative fancy is deliberately blurred in language shorn of concrete spatial and temporal references; here, dream becomes something like a vision born of an active creative will under the mesmeric attraction of an ideal or an image. Finally, on the analogical level, all mental phenomena which share the intensity of a vivid dream are part and parcel of a dreaming process: the momentary reliving of time-past, particularly the tender moments, and the periodic "dreaming" of time-future. To Kung, all is dream—except the *awareness* of it.

When the dream motif operates on the factual level, the dream itself is portrayed as a chance encounter, a moment of revelation lifted out of the context of mortal time and space:

To the tune of "Autumn in the Cassia Hall"

On the ninth day of the sixth month, I dreamed of arriving at a place where beautiful trees flanked cloud-filled verandas, and the scent of lotus permeated palatial halls on a surrounding lake. Deep in their seclusion of mist and breeze, the majestic buildings glistened in towering glory. It was nighttime. Under the broken rays of the moon, one could see about a hundred paces away the water vapor floating in a hazy expanse of green, beyond which stretched the cool, indistinct landscape, layer after innumerable layer. Someone told me, "This is the Hall of Splendor." After I awoke, I recalled the dream and wrote two stanzas about it.[9]

> Outside the moonlight,
> A cleansed world;
> Immortal Isle reposes in deep seclusion.
> From the highest heaven, a silver stream
> Flows past the red wall; no one in sight.
>
> Startled, awake,
> In the dense moonlight;
> A heavenly breeze ferries the bell of dawn.
> Henceforth, to seek again the Hall of Splendor
> How many thousand layers of vermilion doors?   [K 551]

To the Tune of "Dreaming of a Beauty"

The sound of a single flute;
Under the drifting brocade clouds, the moonlight
    seems warm on the jasper balustrade.
A hundred feet of the Milky Way snatched
    and tossed at the ethereal gate;
From hazy windows of the moon palace,
Vibrating in succession in the spring sky,
Come the celestial notes.
Announcement by the lady-in-waiting—
The silken shade suddenly lifted.

Abruptly, sounds
Of the Green Phoenix alighting on the West Pond[10]
And reporting outside the curtain;
Its pendants tinkle faintly.
It knows no human words;
How would the world know?
At the waking moment,
A handful of spring stars overflowing.   [K 551–52]

There are structural and thematic affinities between these two poems. Both contain two separate parts: the dream proper and an afterthought. The first part begins and ends abruptly and is full of sensory details. The second part is further divided into a description of the moment upon waking and a reflective question on the vanished experience, although not necessarily in that order. Thematically, both dreams actualize the ideal of perfection: the magic land and the ideal union. The two dreams, in fact, may be perceived as two stages in the quest for ideal union, whereby the first dream realizes the setting for the second dream, which is the consummation of a clandestine, almost archetypal, love.

The first dream is charged with cinematic impact and lasts only a fleeting moment. The architectural splendor of the Immortal Isle is revealed like a miracle in a flood of moonlight, an awesome scene frozen in boundless space and boundless time. The "red wall" hints at desire and frustration, a tonal discord openly stated in the reflective question at the end. The Hall of Splendor where the Fair One resides, is encased behind layers of "vermilion doors," doors which bar the dreamer.

The second dream finds the dreamer inside fairyland; and the wishes and desires of the first dream are actualized in an environment where everything is kinetic and alive with sound and color. During this part of the dream, the poetic language brims with sensuous imagery ("warm" moonlight, "brocade clouds," "ethereal gate," etc.). With the arrival of the Green Phoenix, the mythological messenger between the human and the celestial worlds, there is a vitiation of the dream's effect; the dreamer begins to wonder if his marvelous love affair will be known to humans. At this point in the poem, the dream proper ends, although it is textually possible to treat the rhetorical question in the third-to-last line as part of the waking reflection. This ambiguity adds to the dream experience a touch of pathos: the courting of ideal beauty is necessarily a secretive and magical affair. Once it is known or transcribed into action, the dream vanishes, only to become in the future a vulgarized tale.[11]

The poet's longing for ideal beauty sometimes appears in the guise of creative fancy. In the following poem, the dream motif is carefully submerged in the density of descriptive minutiae:

> To the tune of "Dreaming of the Lotus"
> —On the same subject—
>
> Back turned to the lamp, phoenix-pillow on its side;
> Before the eye, a pearly beauty flirts with autumn:
> Watery skirt, wind-blown hair.
> Languid dewdrops
> Descend like graceful shadows.
> Infinite, shimmering,
> The moonlight falls on golden ripples far away.
> Standing briefly by the empty pond,
> She complains that her red dress is half-stripped
> And the night chill is piercing.
>
> A pair of mandarin ducks sound asleep in the silence;
> Suddenly, wakened by the falling of seed-cases from the lotus.
> A thick fragrance in the light mist
> Secretly reflects a deep sorrow.
> The soul chills at daybreak;
> Ask not why the verses halt with varied dawn.
> Perhaps the cold makes her shed her pendants;
> And the waves may wet her stockinged feet:[12]
> From without the pond, gusts of morning wind.   [K 541]

Despite the conspicuous title, this dream piece differs from the first two in significant ways. The mute scene of the first dream and the climactic moment of the second are here replaced by a slow hypnotic recounting of a mental phenomenon. The dream does not begin with the first line, nor does it break off clearly anywhere in the poem. Throughout the poem, description mixes with fancy, and mood intrudes upon scene. The end result is an enigmatic piece halfway between factual account and dreamy vision.

The first line supposedly introduces the dream and, therefore, serves a function similar to that of the authorial note to the first poem. Yet, far from clarifying the nature of the forthcoming experience, the "phoenix-pillow on its side" phrase sets off an ambiguous note which is to persist throughout the poem. Since tipping a pillow suggests either a state of sound sleep or insomnia, what follows may belong equally well to the dreamland or to the environment surrounding the insomniac. The textual ambiguity seems to be deliberate. For, swiftly, a picture is conjured up "before the eye" and sustained through seventeen lines of continuous exposure.

The most prominent object in the picture is a lotus flower; it is personified from the beginning and gradually "made" into a true human form by way of empathetic imagination. She is seen as undressing involuntarily during the course of the night. Her "watery skirt" and "wind-blown hair" above the "golden ripples" soon give way to half-nakedness and finally to sorry deciduousness (shedding her "pendants") with the coming of cold dawn. The element of empathy is further underscored by three obscure lines before the dreamer's final reflection on the flower's drooping helplessness. The "deep sorrow" and the soul that "chills at daybreak" are as likely to be those of the creative dreamer as those of the imaginary flower. The creative act ceases as the object of its imagination fades into prosaic daylight.

If the first two dream poems capture a moment of ecstasy during the poet-dreamer's perennial search for ideal beauty, this fanciful piece registers beauty in full flesh and slow motion. Underneath its sensual language, the dream contains a mournful note and some dark hints of the hazards of wakeful reality.

II *Dreamland Revisited*

In the previous poems, dream occurs as part of a present experience and occupies most of the narrative space of the poem.

There is another kind of dream poem in Kung's *tz'u* lyrics in which the memory of dreams is an inexhaustible source of creative inspiration; the description of the dream itself, however, is kept to a minimum. In these poems, dreaming is a prolonged and painstaking act of remembering. Here are two examples:

> To the tune of "Waves Washing over Sand"
> —On a dream—
>
> A good dream is the hardest to retain;
> It whiffs past Immortal Isle,
> And enters the heart intact every time one seeks.
> Leaving without a trace—seeking as usual:
> The high red chamber.
>
> There, the exchange of intimate words;
> The lamplight; the hanging screen—
> Is it heaven? Is it fantasy? Is it love?
> Now, I grieve alone and try to occupy myself,
> So I fabricate this parting sorrow.   [K 545]

> To "The Long Tune on the Magnolia Blossom"
>
> What in both heaven and the human world
> Is the most airy,
> The most listless,
> Perhaps the hardest to express,
> Surely detected by no one,
> Just to be sought quietly, alone?
> A spray of orchid, so fragrant, so slender:
> Why does the fragrant orchid accompany the chanting
>   of this lean verse,
> And suffer this indulgence in sorrow,
> Solemnly, solemnly, till the end of heaven and earth?
>
> Into the orchid lapel
> Drops a cool moon,
> Like a person's heart.
> A dream to be softly, softly told,
> Midst wreaths and wreaths of incense smoke,
> With deep, deep, knitted brow:

A promise in the blue sky to an old friend
To return to heaven and tend the heavenly zither.*
But ever since waking from the dream of the
    immortal realm,
Blue clouds have been hanging low.

*In a dream, I received and read a volume of *tz'u*. Someone told me, "These are
the musical scores for the zither in heaven." [K 546]

In both poems, the dream motif is low-keyed, camouflaged in
soft-spoken language occasionally bordering on obscurantism.
Compared with the previous dream poems, these two lack imagistic
sharpness. Both begin with a leisurely reflection on the nature of
dream and memory, and conclude with a statement about the ir-
revocability of the bright spots in a person's past experience.
Sandwiched in between the leisurely narratives are the bright spots
which have provided the basis for these dreamy reflections. Although these bright spots make only brief cameo-like appearances in
the poems, they prove to be the stuff these dream poems are made
of.

The bright spot in the first poem is the "high red chamber" with
its cozy lamplight and love-nest atmosphere; its sudden appearance
in the middle of a leisurely narrative signals the arrival of the keynote. The rest of the poem diverges from this central image and
ends on a bitter-sweet note: an intense moment in poetic creation is
but a facsimile, a "fabrication" of real sorrow.

This theme of memory and dream as poetic fabrication is mirrored
in the narrative technique of the second poem. While the red
chamber scene partitions the first poem into three parts—the
leisurely reflection, the bright spot, and the concluding
statement—the narrative of the second poem refuses to come into
clear focus until the very end; the casual mention of the "old friend"
and the "heavenly zither" renders the previous section, sixteen lines
long, a rambling soft-keyed prelude. This impressionistic approach
is technically appropriate here. Like the musical scores mentioned
in the footnote, these preludial lines are positioned in the poem to
create an effect similar to that of music. With opaque images and
associated sounds, they evoke a mood which anticipates the
enigmatic "promise" toward the end. Therefore, like the "wreaths
and wreaths of incense smoke," they slowly "fabricate" a dream out
of words.

Creative energy aside, what is the bright moment ladled out of the sea of memory? It is, to paraphrase the poems themselves, a tender scene inside a red chamber and a meeting with an old acquaintance. The good dreams, those "hardest to retain," those recreatable only in words, are in essence dreams of love and friendship: dreams of attachment. The motif of dream as attachment and creative play is openly stated in the first poem in the triple question after the description of the red chamber. In this rhetorical question, dream ("heaven"), creativity ("fantasy"), and love are presented as three possible faces of the same reality.

That Kung Tzu-chen treated the dream motif philosophically is evident from the care he took in grouping his *tz'u* poems. All of the five dream pieces we have examined come from the same collection first entitled *Hung Ch'an* ("Red Dhyāna"), later changed to *Wu-cho* ("Unfettered"). Both *ch'an* and *wu-cho* are Buddhist terms connoting the idea of freedom and liberty gained by a mind or consciousness not in bondage to earthly things. Small wonder then that poems in this collection often revolve around the metaphor of the mind as the reservoir of creative dreams. Whether partial revelation or total fabrication, these creative dreams are the products of a vigilant spirit in constant search of richer experiences and higher ideals. They are, so to speak, free manifestations of *ch'ing* (positive desires), self-generating and ahistorical. Viewed in this perspective, *wu-cho* is a superb title for a group of testimonial poems. By his choice of title, Kung Tzu-chen demonstrated his seriousness in treating the *tz'u* genre. With Kung's other collections, dreams begin to have an anchor in definite historical and personal contexts. And the poems in these collections progressively become more conventional in theme and subject matter.

III   *The Weeping Willow*

One of the key themes in Kung's other *tz'u* collections is the role memory plays in reconciling two orders of time: the irretrievable time experienced by man, and the cyclical time evinced by the regenerative process of nature. Just as dreaming creates for the dreamer a perennial present, memory retrieves the wakeful man from the continuum of time by bracketing off a few treasured moments from its unceasing flow. Both are, as Kung Tzu-chen would have it, the lyrical defense of a sentient being, otherwise lost in "*kalpas* of rebirths."

Man's relationship with nature and time is a highly conventional theme in Chinese poetry. Generally, this theme has been treated in two divergent ways: one naturalistic, the other transcendental. The naturalistic outlook views the schism between the resurgent course of nature and the finite existence of man as an indomitable circumstance, and the awareness of this schism a sorrowful phenomenon. The only relief a vigilant mind can hope for in the face of death and indifferent time is by way of emotional extravagance. One recalls the hilarious drinking songs of a Li Po (701–62), the elegiac exuberance of a Su Shih (1037–1101), and the heroic rantings of a Hsin Ch'i-chi (1140–1207), to name just a few of the major voices. Together these voices constitute a poetic tradition which may perhaps be called "carpe diem": live and let live while there is time, for tomorrow all will be reduced to "smoke and ashes."[13]

The transcendental treatment of the theme of nature and man, on the other hand, revolves around the Buddho-Taoist notion of universal harmony, ever since these two attitudes of life converged and took hold of Chinese literary consciousness during the Six Dynasties (4th–6th cent. A.D.). It is essentially a poetic reflection of a lyrical, holistic mode of perception which regards man and nature as inseparable parts of an organic universe. It is man's lot to be an integral part of nature and a passing phenomenon of history; and it is his duty as well as privilege not to disrupt this universal scheme. In fact, with a touch of imagination or intellectual maturity, the poetic mind can even derive some quiet pleasure in understanding its own finality in a world of seemingly unchanging things. Viewed from a transcendental point of view, all is matter and change; all is mind and permanence. Change and permanence are but variant categories of thought devised by man to cope with a phenomenal universe. So too are joys and sorrows, the price man pays for taking experiences too literally. Such lyrical forms of thought, a mixture of Buddhist resignation and Taoist exultation over nature, has left its imprint on many a poetic expression since the "Nature Poets" of the Six Dynasties. It found its most articulate spokesman in the T'ang master Wang Wei (699–759), whose quiet lines often bear witness to a serene mind which perceives the human and the natural worlds with equal equanimity. His poems can capture the nuances of a landscape without the intrusion of an assertive mind. They describe a nature which is in mutual communion with man instead of being the cause for hedonistic abandonment.

In Kung Tzu-chen's treatment of this conventional theme, we hear a different voice in his *tz'u* from that in his *shih* poems. As stated earlier, Kung as a *shih* poet, particularly in the regimented *chüeh-chü* form, was very much influenced by the Buddhist doctrine of "emptiness" *(k'ung)*, although he seldom dealt with the theme of man and nature directly. It is, therefore, interesting to note that in his *tz'u* poems, he treated the theme not only with vivid descriptiveness but also with palpable emotion. In some of his *tz'u*, the intellect's acceptance of things as they are yields to a flamboyant display of wishful imagination—for example, in the previous dream poems—and also to a deep grief over the mutability of human relations and of all things in nature; nature and the external world are thus no longer the subject of thought but have become sharply defined objects of observation and remembrance. The external world is now the arena of change where the compliant human "lovers" come and go.

> To the tune of "Moon on the Hsiang River"
> —Boating on West Lake in the spring of Chia-hsü [1814]—
>
> Lake clouds like dreams—
> Remembering this place from the year before last:
> That weeping willow where the horse was tied.
> An expanse of snail-green spring hills
> Frown at me; beautiful, coquettish.
> The fragrant soul of Little Su,[14]
> The short-lived ambition of Prince Ch'ien[15]—
> Dexterous brushes have portrayed them through the years;
> And in this home-country,
> How many names live on like theirs?
>
> A serious and deft man I have always been;
> If the bygone heroes arose,
> Whose arm would they take?
> The questioned mountain-spirits do not answer;
> Just me, pacing at their feet.
> Dark grass touches the sky,
> Green shade trails the passerby;
> Slowly, slowly, soon, early summer—
> Time drifts casually.
> For now, thoroughly carefree.   [K 565]

This poem comes from the collection entitled, very appropriately, *Lyrics from the Hall of Remembrance*. The subtitle gives the date of 1814. Two years earlier, the poet had married his first wife. West Lake was the site where the young couple went boating together the summer after their wedding. In the following year (1813), the bride died—she was only twenty-two.[16] Even if we did not have this biographical information, the theme of memory as the catalyst of powerful emotions would still be unmistakable. In revisiting the scenic spot, the poet contrasts the fact that the place remains unchanged ("this place . . . / That weeping willow") with the great changes in his own life. He recalls that history has swept away many kindred souls from the scene; only a fortunate few have survived in poetry. There is clearly a schism between everlasting nature and the precarious existence of man, a schism which can only be healed by the grace of memory. Yet the poetic mind is too sensitive to tarry in the land of personal past. Rather, it dwells on the beauty of the "spring hills" and the romantic biographies of some "home-country" historical figures. In the concluding lines, the poet makes a casual reference to the coming of summer and resolves to be "thoroughly carefree," although at the back of his mind he knows that soon another spring will be over, like many of the previous springs which have rushed away taking with them the "fragrant soul of Little Su" and the "short-lived ambition of Prince Ch'ien."

This contrived nonchalance makes the poem a good example of what traditional critics cherished as *ch'en yü* (sedimental/suppressed grief). *Ch'en yü* is a quality which is applicable to both the way in which profound emotions are presented and the powerful effect these emotions have on the reader. The main purpose of *ch'en yü* is to prevent a poem with a tense emotional structure from becoming bathetic. And *ch'en yü* is inseparable from the organization of the poem. In the present case, the poet creates the effect of understated sorrow by introducing a series of emotional episodes which he checks before they have a chance to overwhelm him with their intensity.

The first emotional episode is an act of recollection; it comes immediately after the one-line preamble "Lake clouds [are] like dreams," which introduces the motif of redemptive memory. This episode itself takes up only two lines, as if the poet is afraid to prolong the painful moment. However, the two sharp images of memory—the weeping willow and the tethered horse—bridge the present and the past and usher in the sub-theme of nature versus history, which lasts through the middle lines up to the moment the poet asks with bravado: "If the bygone heroes arose, / Whose arm would they take?" This bravado marks the second emotional episode which is immediately held in check by a swift change of subject and mood. Instead of pondering the fate of heroes past, the poet returns to the present scene with all its charm of a mellowed spring. The idea of onrushing time is suggested by the "dark grass" and the "green shade" which herald the approach of summer. The past is bygone, the present is continually changing, and nature (the "mountain-spirits") is mute; toward what can one aspire but care-freeness even if just "for now"? This brief final line is the third and last emotional episode; its conciliatory tone makes it all the more poignant. *Ch'en yü,* the art of understated grief, has found a proper demonstration in what is unquestionably one of Kung's best *tz'u* poems.

The muffled grief of "Moon on the Hsiang River" is echoed in some poems in which the idea of two kinds of time is presented in almost pure imagistic terms. For example:

To the tune of "The Flower-Seller's Song"
—Observations on passing by White Gate [Nanking] in a boat—

Sails billow with mist at the southern capital.
The past seems near when one looks back.
West of the red wall stretches Little Ch'ang-kan Lane,
Where once a pretty maid of fifteen
Filled the wine-shop with spring.

Such are the hills from the Six Dynasties.
The crow-black hair has worn away;
The flowers in the rain and the clouds of leaves
     are wasted now.
A hundred miles of river-sound rushes on with a dream:
When will I return?   [K 561]

To the tune of "The Divination Song"

Once, beside a curved railing,
A glimpse of a thin silk skirt;
Tiny steps turned back in the laced shadows of flowers;
Moonlit curtains parted.

> Still the same curved railing,
> Memory of her graceful form;
> In *kalpas* of rebirths, hardly a second meeting—
> An image sealed in the heart.   [K 577]

Like "Moon on the Hsiang River," these two poems are struc-tured around the dichotomy of time (fluidity and change) and place (stability and permanence) with an implied theme of man as the hapless eyewitness of history and change. In all three poems the sense of irreparable loss and subsequent grief is activated by the presence of some familiar scenes which remind the poet of the ravages of time. However, the scenes which engender the sequence of emotions—remembrance, grief, and final consolation—are de-picted from different perspectives.

In "Moon on the Hsiang River," the poet's vision of the physical scene triggers the release of his grief over a recent personal loss ("Remembering this place from the year before last"). "The Flower-Seller's Song," on the other hand, contains scenes and flashbacks from the "Six Dynasties" and this implicitly telescopes the rise and fall of those short-lived dynasties. Each poem en-compasses a progressively greater interval of time; indeed, the last poem concludes with the Buddhist metaphor of the world as a stage for "*kalpas* of rebirths," a somnolent course of time which engulfs the artificial divisions of past, present, and future. With each shift of conceptual vantage point, the elegiac poet becomes more pensive and less anguished. What begins as a counsel to himself to momentarily forget the human plight in unsympathetic nature ("The questioned mountain-spirits do not answer") eventually mellows into a quiet affirmation that the image-making capacity of mind and memory ("An image sealed in the heart") can both counteract in-eluctable mutability and prevent any loss from being final. Memory is therefore not only a catalyst of powerful emotions but also a balm capable of healing the wounds of loss and bereavement.

The shift of tone from protective self-counsel to affirmation is achieved through a manipulation of the descriptive-reflective approach used in some of the dream poems discussed earlier. The strength of this approach lies in the delicate balance of imagery and ideas; for example, in the two poems cited above, the first stanzas consist of lines made mostly of images; the second stanzas then "dilute" the imagistic intensity with reflective statements. The two halves thus complement each other: the compact imagery provides a sensory correlative to the reflective ideas, vivifying them; the reflections, on the other hand, add a semantic structure to and suggest a philosophical purpose for the sensory details embodied in the imagery.

"The Flower-Seller's Song" opens with two pairs of antithetic images: the static "southern capital" contrasts with the wind-borne "sails," symbol of mobility and change; and the silent "Little Ch'ang-kan Lane," the historic site of wine-shops in the past, is juxtaposed with "a pretty maid of fifteen" who once had enlivened the drinking scenes with her girlish charms ("spring"). Human beings, like wind-borne sails, come and go, while the river remains forever. The dual nature of time (stasis versus change) embodied in the imagery of the first stanza is elaborated in the second, the reflective portion of the poem. The poet sorrowfully reflects that in the due course of time all "crow-black hair" will wear away; even the present flash of feelings will soon fade into the bulging past ("A hundred miles of river-sound rushes on"), awaiting the summons of another "dream."

The same kind of progression from the visual to the cerebral characterizes "The Divination Song." A quick succession of sharp images comprises the first stanza: a curved railing, a corner of a silk skirt, retreating steps, flower shadows, and parted curtains under the moonlight. The only nonimagistic words in this section are the temporal referent *ts'eng* (once upon a time) and the verbal construction *p'ieh chien* (saw in a glance), part of the sense of which is sacrificed in translation. The rapidity with which these images assult the senses recalls the opening lines of "Dreaming of a Beauty," in which the dreamer finds himself in an empyrean setting brimming with sound and color. The similarity, however, lies only in the compact imagery involved. The atmosphere of "The Divination Song" lacks the sense of joy and wonder which denotes the fulfillment of love. The scene here is hushed and eerie, as if resurrected from a pristine past. But with the parting of the curtains, the first stanza comes to an abrupt end. Memory has performed its wonder in defying time. But what for?

The second stanza recapitulates portions of the remembered scene; but the language is now philosophical: despite the law of recurrence ("*kalpas* of rebirths"), the "graceful" person who once brightened the familiar landscape will never be encountered again.

Endless time is a vast and somber shadow in which human beings and human experiences emerge briefly: a moment lost is a moment lost forever, save perhaps through the intervention of redemptive memory. Although human experiences form a string of losses, although the two orders of time, as suggested by "the same railing," are indomitable, man can at least diminish the pain of loss by memory. And remembering, like dreaming, is an image-making process. The pictorial nature of memory can prevent the "graceful form" of past experience from vanishing into infinite darkness.

IV   *The Tower and the Lake*

Finally, dream can be the unpretentious daydreaming which every person of *ch'ing* ("lover" in Kung's terminology) resorts to when external events in life have become too disappointing and the creative self is no longer capable of maintaining a proper emotional distance from his art. As a result, the poet may come dangerously close to making plain statements of his personal interests.

In the two examples below, the tower and the lake are obviously a projection of the ailing traveler's yearning for some emotional anchorage outside the confines of the lonely self:

To the tune of "The Divination Song"

There is a tall tower by the river;
Is it as secluded as the tower by the lake?
Beyond that tower, gentle ripples extend, layer after layer,
Retaining not even the shadow of the startled wild goose.

Duckweed leaves flirt with the setting sun;
Orchid buds wilt in the bright mirror.
Nipping all the autumn flowers, the coldness spreads,
    wave after wave,
While someone lies ill south of the river.   [K 574]

To the tune of "Waves Washing over Sand"
—Wishes—

A vermilion tower rises beyond the clouds,
Enshrined in mist, cool and secluded;
Flute songs puncture the autumn air of the Five Lakes.
Gathering my paintings and scripts, thirty thousand scrolls,
We shall board the magnolia boat.

The mirror stand, the incense brazier,
Elegant, tranquil, gentle.
Carefully, carefully hook up the curtains for me.
Ignoring the rippling lake and the fresh lake breeze,
I shall watch you tend your hair.   [K 571]

The first piece is from the *Lyrics of Minor Tranquility,* a collection of reflective verses on miscellaneous topics. The second piece
comes from the *Lyrics of Allusion,* which describe the slow
metamorphosis of the relationship between the poet and a courtesan
from a trysting to a lasting one. The poems herein are arranged in a
sequence with recurrent geographical references to the region of
the Five Lakes, the poet's home-country. Yet despite the poet's
classificatory preferences, the two pieces cited above are related in
both imagery and personae. The ailing traveler of the first piece
longs to be the poet-recluse of the second.

The emotional nadir of the ailing traveler and his vision of a better
future ("wishes") are linked by two clusters of images and a
hypothetical journey. The first group of images gravitates around
the "river," conventional Chinese symbol of continuous change; the
second group is assimilated into the "lake," which contextually
suggests home and security. Associated with the river are
duckweeds, the setting sun, wilting flowers, and the bedridden
wanderer; associated with the lake are flute songs, refreshing
breezes, and two standard props in a tranquil domestic setting: a
mirror stand and an incense brazier. Superimposed on the two sets
of images is the tower, a temporary shelter for the traveler in the
first piece, a fortress of love in the second. The distance between the
two towers is traversed by a hypothetical "magnolia boat"; this
journey, however, as the poet says in the subtitle, is only in a
daydream.

It is life in the second tower that the dejected traveler in the first
tower yearns for: a naturalized version of life in the dreamland
where only flute songs intrude upon the privacy of the lovers; except
that this idyllic mode of life is cast in subjunctive language. What
the dreamer of Immortal Isle can summon with an act of joyous
imagination, the run-of-the-mill natural man can now only entertain
as "wishes," something he clings to as a reprieve from the
harassment of daily life. It is interesting to compare the last scene of
the second poem with a similiar setting in the Chi-hai quatrain
which we analyzed in some detail under the idea of *han-hsü* (poetic

economy and suggestiveness). In the *chüeh-chü,* the woman rolls up the screen of the boudoir to remind the poet of the rolling Yellow River and his erstwhile socio-political commitments. In the *tz'u,* the curtains are "carefully, carefully" hooked up to give on a secluded lake, showing the poet's willingness, in fact eagerness, to subject ambition to the tempering quality of love.

The subjective sentiments which are partially objectified in the imagery of the previous daydreams come to the fore in the following *tz'u:*

> To the tune of "Gold Thread Song"
> —For Scholar Li—
>
> Like clouds and duckweeds on the sea, we met.
> Laughable! All these years we talked about sword-play
>   while drinking,
> Or climbed a high tower to discuss rhyme-prose.
> A myriad of flowers madly in bloom pass like a dream;
> And even in the dream, flowers are no more than mist:
> What will they be to the wakeful eye?
> Already, I alone am wakeful and unused to wakefulness.
> Why did I not spend my gold on songs and dances instead?
> Outside the moonlight,
> Bitter thoughts.
>
> Unusual talent does not always make heaven jealous;
> Only your ancestor of the joined eyebrows and long nails
> Died young by chance.
> Such beautiful moonlit flowers on the lakeside hills!
> Who is there to enjoy them in this transient existence?
> Do not be angry with a word of advice:
> Give up your mad ways while there is time;
> Frosty hair announces the coming of middle age.
> Keep me company;
> Stay in Buddha's light.   [K 564]
>
> To the tune of "The Ugly Slave"
>
> Pondering the events of fifteen years,
> The floods of talent,
> The floods of tears:
> A failure in both the flute-like sentiment and the
>   swordsman's fame.

> Not a single dream of interest in spring;
> I repent my roving,
> I refute my roving:
> Witness the gold-lettered Sutra by my pillow.   [K 577]

The first piece registers in musical and yet abstract language the poet's disenchantment with life at the approach of middle age: behind him is a youth ill-spent in ambition and self-indulgence ("sword-play" and "rhyme-prose"); before him lurks the threat of untimely death, a motif embedded in the allusion to the T'ang poet Li Ho ("your ancestor of the joined eyebrows and long nails"), who died in his twenties. Alone and sober, the logical outcome of a life of abstraction, the poet pleads for deliverance from loneliness in friendship and higher dreams (transcendental contemplation).

The second piece pursues the poet's renunciation with incantatory lines; it seems as if the poet tries to induce the man cursed with sobriety ("I alone am wakeful") to forget and to sleep. The lines are dotted with personal references ("the flute-like sentiment and the swordsman's fame"); the emotions are powerful but somewhat uncoordinated and desultory. The poet has stayed too close to his personal experience to dress ideas in the tapestry of artistic dreams. In his eagerness to express the natural self, he has adopted a voice which traditional critics refer to as *hao fang* (romantic/heroic abandon).

Seventeen years later, in a fifth and last *tz'u* collection entitled simply *Keng-tzu ya-tz'u* (*The Elegant Lyrics of the Year Keng-tzu* [1840]), a similar "heroic voice" in an identical prosodic pattern speaks:

> To the tune of "The Ugly Slave"
> —In answer to an outing invitation of two friends[17]—

> Former haunts revisited after twenty-five years:
> This faintly familiar river,
> These faintly familiar hills;
> The grave, heroic ambitions of youth unfulfilled.

> The poets ask me why I return.
> Too forlorn for verse,
> Too forlorn for words—
> Let me just carry the sunset of past dynasties home.   [K 583–84]

The tune is a superb choice. Its prosodic features, notably the parallel middle lines of each stanza, lend themselves to the mood of recurrent thoughts and sentiments; many poets in fact have favored this tune. And with the reference to poets and the idea of "return," we shall now go back to literary tradition to see how Kung Tzu-chen relates to his fellow dreamers.

V *Tradition and Synthesis*

T'an Hsien (1832–1901), a leading *tz'u* poet-critic of the Ch'ing dynasty, offered the following comment on Kung Tzu-chen's *tz'u* from the perspective of literary tradition: "His *tz'u* are downy and ornate *(mien li)* as well as ponderous and soaring *(ch'en yang)*, as though fusing Chou [Pang-yen] and Hsin [Ch'i-chi] into one; truly unique pieces."[18] Like most general statements, this remark is illuminating on the one hand and, on the other, descriptively inadequate and imprecise. Since the two Sung masters Chou Pang-yen (1057–1121) and Hsin Ch'i-chi traditionally represent the two dominant strands of the art of *tz'u* writing,[19] T'an Hsien's "fusing" amounts to an unreserved compliment: Kung Tzu-chen's *tz'u* span the stylistic spectrum from the delicate artistry *(wan yüeh)* of Chou Pang-yen to the romantic abandon *(hao fang)* of Hsin Ch'i-chi; in other words, his poetry incorporates the best elements of the *tz'u* tradition into a personal and synthetic whole. The validity of this observation is generally borne out by a quick comparison of such tonally different poems as the "Dreaming of a Beauty" and the "Gold Thread Song," both translated and discussed earlier. However, T'an Hsien does not tell us precisely how Kung Tzu-chen's *tz'u* resemble those of his precursors, and in what ways they are "unique." In the following pages, we shall consider the question of tradition versus individual synthesis by first comparing Kung Tzu-chen with Chou Pang-yen and Hsin Ch'i-chi, and then with his contemporary *tz'u* poets.

On the whole, the examples selected in this chapter tend to stress the *mien li* (downy and ornate) side of Kung Tzu-chen. The dream pieces, in particular, call for comparison with Chou Pang-yen, a master craftsman renowned for his polished diction and assiduous attention to descriptive details. The stylistic similarities between Kung and Chou, however, begin and end with their fondness for sensuous and elegant language. A closer comparison shows that

Kung differs from Chou in several significant aspects: (1) Chou Pang-yen excels in close observation and precise description of objects, whether indoor or outdoor, whereas Kung Tzu-chen rarely records objects at close range; (2) Chou devotes many of his long tunes to the recording of events associated with specific occasions such as parting, revisitation of an old site, or a rendezvous, while Kung generally favors a more introspective treatment of similar topics; his is seldom a straightforward narrative approach; and (3) Chou, who had served at the *Ta-sheng Fu* (the government Music Bureau of Sung times) with distinction, is considered exemplary in his flawless application of *tz'u* prosodies; Kung, on the other hand, often deviates from the prescribed tune patterns and is well known for being prosodically unconventional.[20] We shall have occasion to return to this last point.

With Hsin Ch'i-chi, the comparison stands on firmer ground. Hsin's *tz'u* poetry is particularly noted for its prose syntax and torrential emotions (*hao fang*); both characteristics are evident to a certain extent in the more vigorous pieces of Kung (e.g., the "Gold Thread Song" and the first "Ugly Slave"). Besides a common soaring style (T'an Hsien's *yang*), the two poets also share in their art the special quality of *ch'en yü*, or understated grief. *Ch'en yü* is a term which, despite frequent use by critics, is hardly ever defined. Therefore, the following passage from Ch'en T'ing-cho's (1853–92) *Pai-yü-chai tz'u-hua* deserves some attention:

In the composition of *tz'u*, the most treasured quality is *ch'en yü* (suppressed grief). If one can *ch'en* (suppress) then one's *tz'u* will not be superficial. If one can *yü* (grieve) then one's *tz'u* will not be frivolous. . . . By *ch'en yü* is meant that a person's volition precedes the brush and his spirit lingers after the words. It expresses the feelings of frustrated men and lovelorn women, the thoughts of unfavored sons and forsaken ministers. The estrangement between friends and the loneliness of a wanderer can all be conveyed through the description of a lone grass and a single tree. And yet such a conveyance has to be indirect and half concealed; it is replete with subtle hints and roundabout references but never explodes out of an explicit statement. This [art of *ch'en yü*] not only represents an outstanding achievement in style but also reflects a personality of great depth.[21]

Both Hsin Ch'i-chi and Kung Tzu-chen at their best evince the quality of *ch'en yü*. For example, the way Kung handles the emotional episodes in "Moon on the Hsiang River" poignantly dem-

onstrates how profound sorrow can be conveyed through under-
statement. It is also interesting to compare the second piece of
Kung's "The Ugly Slave" with a famous piece by Hsin Ch'i-chi to the
same tune: "In my youth, not knowing the taste of sorrow, / I loved
to climb a storeyed tower . . ."[22] In both instances, the poets express a wordless sorrow over the inexorable passage of life; while the
one refrains from overt lamentation by changing the subject to the
coolness of autumn, the other avoids a direct comment on his mental despondency by shifting his attention to the sunset.

While T'an Hsien's "ponderous and soaring" is generally an
accurate description of both Hsin Ch'i-chi and Kung Tzu-chen, it
would be erroneous to assume that resemblance in overall style
entails resemblance in technical detail. Even in his more vigorous
pieces, where the lines generally follow the straightforward word
order of prose, Kung never goes so far as to incorporate entire prose
sentences from classical sources verbatim into his text, something
Hsin did frequently. Nor is Kung as fond of using literary and historical allusions as Hsin.[23] These technical differences are illuminating, especially when we recall that, in the *shih* form, Kung is
rather liberal with his use of erudite allusions and archaic expressions; sometimes he seems to tease the reader deliberately with
strange or unexpected words. In Kung's *tz'u*, however, it is the
unhindered flow of feeling that matters.

The foregoing comparisons, hopefully, have demonstrated the
inherent weaknesses of a critical approach which categorizes poets
with traditional terms such as *mien li* and *ch'en yang*. These generally impressionistic terms are vague and amorphous concepts which
do no more than suggest a poet's stylistic features and affinities. In
T'an Hsien's usage, *mien li* echoes the loaded *wan yüeh* and more or
less means softness and richness of texture, density of descriptive
minutiae, refined sentiments, and so forth, for all of which Chou
Pang-yen is considered an exemplary master; *ch'en yang*, on the
other hand, recalls the term *hao fang*, which is frequently used to
suggest untrammeled emotion, torrential rhetoric, and fluctuating
rhythm, supposedly characteristic of Hsin Ch'i-chi's *tz'u* poetry at
its most representative. Therefore, when he compares Kung Tzu-
chen with the Sung masters, T'an Hsien shows the traditional critic's
predilection for grouping poets in terms of stylistic affinities rather
than on their individual merits. This practice of categorizing is part
of the preoccupation with tradition, a preoccupation which is a

recurrent phenomenon in the history of Chinese verse. During the Ch'ing period, tradition practically became the predominant concern, touching the *tz'u* genre as well as others.

The history of Ch'ing *tz'u* is a series of aesthetic reactions toward the question of tradition and imitation: in other words, what should constitute the mainstream of poetic inspiration? There is a historical factor at work: the *tz'u* genre had already degenerated into a decadent and frivolous form of art in the hands of the Ming practitioners;[24] therefore, from the very start, the *tz'u* poets of Ch'ing times looked over the shoulders of their mediocre Ming predecessors to the Sung period (generally considered to be the "Golden Age" of *tz'u*) and even beyond. They were anxious, both in theory and in practice, to revive and enrich the *tz'u* form with fresh themes and purposes; they hoped to elevate its status with technical triumphs worthy of the distinguished Sung poets. However, although they wanted to rejuvenate the form, the Ch'ing poet-critics disagreed strongly on what represented the main tradition and who, of the pre-Ming masters, provided the ideal models for imitation. Their differences became so great that it has become customary for literary historians to survey the field of Ch'ing *tz'u* in terms of "schools," and to treat individual *tz'u* poets in terms of their respective places within each school, often with contradictory results. Kung Tzu-chen, for instance, has been assigned to both of the leading schools.[25]

Generally speaking, the story of Ch'ing *tz'u* is the story of the interreactions among three schools, each with a proposed creative ideal and a set of critical principles, and each hoping to reaffirm the status of the *tz'u*. (There were, of course, *tz'u* poets who wrote independently of any school; such towering figures as Nara Singde [1655–85] and Chiang Ch'un-lin [1818–68] retained their individual voices above the storm of theoretical controversies.[26]) Chronologically, the first two schools—"Yang-hsien" and "Che-hsi," named after a county in modern Kiangsu and the western part of Chekiang province, respectively—emerged almost simultaneously in the mid-seventeenth century; the loyalties of minor *tz'u* poets were divided between the two for a while, until finally the Che-hsi School prevailed over its rival and won acclaim as the standard-bearer for the restoration of the *tz'u*. Thereafter, the Che-hsi poets dominated the *tz'u* world for over a century; not until the emergence of a third school—"Ch'ang-chou," named after a prefecture in modern

Kiangsu—in the late eighteenth century did their influence begin to wane. The subsequent period of Ch'ing *tz'u* is historically viewed as a reaction to the joint impact of the Che-hsi and the Ch'ang-chou schools, especially the latter.[27] And Kung Tzu-chen, writing in the nineteenth century, is consequently taken to be part of that reaction.

What were the distinctive features of each school and what were the central issues at stake? To answer this question properly, we have to separate theory from practice and examine them individually. In terms of practice, all three schools wanted to eschew the decadence of Ming and return to the vigorous tradition of Sung. To the Yang-hsien group, headed by Ch'en Wei-sung (1625–82) and his brothers, the glory of Sung *tz'u* lay in the spontaneous revelation of personality and powerful feelings so aptly done by Su Shih and Hsin Ch'i-chi; and to revive the *tz'u* was to imitate the *hao fang* of Su and Hsin.[28] The Che-hsi poets, on the other hand, saw the quintessence of *tz'u* in the painstaking craftsmanship and the mellowed sentiments of the less "heroic" poets. However, there was a slight disagreement among the Che-hsi poets as to which Sung masters provided the best model for imitation. Chu I-tsun (1629–1709), the "founder" of the school, recommended the Southern Sung poets, Chiang K'uei (1155?–1235?) and Chang Yen (1248–1320?) in particular; Li O (1692–1752), the most astute critic and easily the best practitioner of the group, singled out Chou Pang-yen as the artist par excellence.[29] The tenets of the Ch'ang-chou school synthesized the Yang-hsien group's adoration of temperament and spontaneity and the Che-hsi poets' preoccupation with form and craftsmanship: poetic practice should be informed by creative ideals, and spontaneity need not sacrifice the maturity of vision. The first idea is embedded in the *i-nei yen-wai* motto ("meaning within, language without," or proper thought dressed in proper language) proposed by Chang Hui-yen (1761–1802), the titular leader of the group; the second idea paraphrases approximately the complex *chi t'o* theory (carrying/conveying messages; multiple meanings) of Chou Chi (1781–1839), whose stature among the Ch'ang-chou group often overshadowed that of Chang Hui-yen.[30] Here, we are already within the confines of literary theory.

If the three schools differed in their creative emphases, they did share one common conviction in theory: *tz'u* had been unfairly relegated to the status of a dispensable minor genre, an offshoot of *shih*, partly due to the ingrained prejudice of early critics, and partly due to the lack of concerted effort on the part of *tz'u* poets to take their craft seriously. The Ch'ing poets tried to elevate the status of the genre *(tsun t'i)*. *Tsun t'i*, or "elevating the genre," is in fact the key term in the history of Ch'ing *tz'u* criticism; practically every critic of interest from the three schools touched upon the ideal of *tsun t'i* at one time or another.

To these critics, the most effective way to dignify a literary genre was to place it upon the pedestal of antiquity. In their theoretical writings, all three schools sought to link the *tz'u* directly with either the *Shih ching (Book of Songs)* or the *Ch'u tz'u (Songs of the South)*, the fountainheads of poetic inspiration. The Yang-hsien School perceived some organic relationships between the *tz'u*, the *feng* (folk songs) section of the *Shih ching*, and the eloquent *sao* style of the *Ch'u tz'u*, taking their affinity with music and their uninhibited demonstration of genuine emotion as the cementing factors.[31] The Che-hsi School also went back to the *Shih ching* for a clue to the origin of *tz'u*, but found it in the *ya* (elegant court songs) section instead of in the *feng*. In the decorous language and orderly presentation of the *ya* poems, they found an echo of their own ideal of *ya cheng* (elegance and propriety).[32] Some Che-hsi poets, Chu I-tsun for one, strained *ya cheng* to the extent that even meticulous attention to prosody and language was not sufficient without the embellishment of scholarship. (The result of this display of scholarship was often a woefully obscure piece of *tz'u* laden with allusions.) Finally, the Ch'ang-chou School, with its late-comer's hindsight, proposed a theory which encompassed both form and content, feeling and thought.

Of all the catchwords in Ch'ing *tz'u* criticism, two of the most suggestive and far-reaching are perhaps Chang Hui-yen's *i-nei yen-wai* and Chou Chi's *chi t'o*. The two terms basically express the same creative ideal—how to best harmonize *i* (thought or tenor) with *yen* (language)—but with different emphases: Chang Hui-yen emphasizes the correctness of message, Chou Chi the multiplicity of poetic meaning. For instance, in the famous anthology *Tz'u hsüan*, a scrupulously selective collection of lyrics covering the period from Late T'ang to Southern Sung, Chang provides the following interpretation of a well-known piece by Su Shih:

. . . "a startled wild goose" means the noble person is ill at ease. "Turning its head" means he still longs after the ruler. "No one notices" means the ruler is unaware. "Scanning all the chilly branches but unwilling to perch on any of them" means he will not occupy high offices idly. "The solitude of a cold sandbank" means he feels unsettled . . . [33]

Here Chang tries to correct the *tz'u's* reputation as a "petty craft" (*hsiao chi* or *hsiao tao*) by reading didactic and allegorical messages into the poems. In his own *tz'u* writing, an example of which will be given later, the allegorical intent is often too obvious.

Chang Hui-yen's emphasis on meaning and message paved the way for the arrival of Chou Chi's comprehensive *chi t'o:*

In learning to compose *tz'u*, a student should aim at having a message (*yu chi t'o*). When there is a message to convey, then the language and the ideas of the *tz'u* will be mutually complementary; and the *tz'u* will be a graceful piece. After one has developed an individual style, one should aim at having no specific messages (*wu chi t'o*). When a *tz'u* is without a specific message, then its reference to events and portrayal of feelings will be open to individual interpretations ("humaneness to the humane and wisdom to the wise"). . . . [34] Without a message, a *tz'u* is superficial (*pu ju*); on the other hand, if bogged down by specific messages, a *tz'u* will not be able to come alive (*pu ch'u*). [35]

Chou Chi gives equal importance to the concerns of the three *tz'u* schools—expression, language, and maturity of thought. Small wonder then that as far as critical theory goes, the *chi t'o* ideal has had a ripple effect on later poetry. The dichotomous emphasis on "having a message" and "having no message" recalls in particular Kung Tzu-chen's description of *ch'ing* in his "Self-Preface": something which suggests "both reality and unreality," something which points out by "not pointing," and something which may be "caused by joy and sorrow" but is not "bound by joy and sorrow." In the same preface, Kung goes on to lament his inability to sustain the ideal of *wu chu* (not abiding) and *wu chi* (no specific referents) in his aesthetic life. The terminology, despite the Buddhist ring (e.g., *wu chu*), is reminiscent of Chou Chi.

Kung seldom theorizes about purely literary matters. The "Self-Preface" to his *tz'u* collection is a rare statement of creative principle; it reads like a direct rebuttal of Chang Hui-yen's advocacy of Confucian ethics. Although Kung generally agrees with Chou Chi's idea of spontaneous message, his dream motif demonstrates that poetic meaning does not have to be accompanied by moral instruction. However, when we turn from theory to practice, we find that Kung shares a number of preferences with the Ch'ang-chou poets. The latter generally shun obscure allusions and pay scant attention to prosodic requirements, for they consider both a hindrance to the expression of ideas; Kung, too, uses allusions only sparingly and is unconventional in his prosody. Let us have an example from Chang Hui-yen for a detailed comparison:

> To "The Long Tune on the Magnolia Blossom"
> —On the willow catkin—

> Though fallen, adrift, nearing its end,
> Who would cherish it as a flower,
> When the wind is turned away by double screens,
> The rain recedes from thick curtains,
> And clouds hover above delicate streamers?[36]
> Searching for its companions in spring,
> It meets, at sunset, with only the scattered petals.
> Still, unable to lie down in silence,
> It flies up again the moment it swirls to the ground.

> By nature unbridled,
> It endures mournfully till the close of spring;
> Only plum blossoms under the moon
> And snowflakes on a wintry day
> Can match its icy purity:
> Now, its intense grievances suppressed,
> It coils round the misty hills all day, like shadows
>   of sadness.
> Look at the green, green duckweed by the pond;
> They are spots of teardrops congealed.[37]

The language of the poem strikes a nice balance between description and ideas; and the metaphorical use of personification is exceptionally effective. With the exception of two short asides, the entire first stanza reads like an on-the-scene report of a trivial incident: a hapless flower's obdurate struggle for survival during a rainstorm. The scene begins to take on meaning for us, however, when we encounter the authorial comments in the second stanza. As a result of the author's consistent use of personification and abstract

terms such as "icy purity" (*ch'ing han*), an inevitable association of
the fate of the flower with something weightier gradually emerges;
this something may well be a person of great strength and character,
a person who can withstand all kinds of weather. But we cannot be
sure. It would be interesting to see the correspondence of verse
with moral precept Chang Hui-yen himself would have offered.

How does this poem compare with Kung Tzu-chen's *tz'u*? First,
on purely technical grounds, both poets employ the same long tune
(Kung's was cited earlier in section II); both violate prosodic rules;[38]
both, especially Kung, are careful with the sense and sound of
language. Secondly, neither poem relies heavily on allusions.
Thirdly, Chang's arrangement of his poem into two clear-cut
divisions—sensory details and authorial comments—recalls Kung's
favorite description-reflection approach.

These technical similarities may suggest that Kung Tzu-chen's
tz'u poems bear the imprint of the Ch'ang-chou style. T'an Hsien,
for instance, has selected Kung for his list of "The Seven Later
Masters" (*hou ch'i-chia*) of Ch'ing *tz'u*, together with such leaders of
the Ch'ang-chou School as Chang Hui-yen, Chou Chi, and Chiang
Tun-fu (1808–67).[39] Kung himself also expressed great admiration
for this group: in "Song on the Talents of Ch'ang-chou" (*Chang-chou
kao-ts'ai p'ien*), he praises its numerous achievements; of their *tz'u*,
he writes:

> Every one excels in the "little song-form":[40]
> Graceful, moving, and resonant.   [K 494]

Among his Ch'ang-chou friends mentioned in the poem, Ting Li-
heng, Yün Ching, Lu Chi-lu and Chang Ch'i, the younger brother of
Chang Hui-yen and the co-compiler of the *Tz'u hsüan*, were all
established *tz'u* authors.[41]

Nevertheless, appreciation does not automatically imply conscious imitation. For Kung differs from Chang Hui-yen in just as
many ways as he resembles him. Kung has a wide range of style and
a poetic voice which encompasses both the hypnotic murmur of
"Dreaming of the Lotus" and the elegiac abandon of "The Ugly
Slave"; Chang's voice, however, is usually the dispassionate, even
tone of the scholar-poet. In addition, Kung's *tz'u* seldom carry heavy
messages, certainly not messages of such gravity as would satisfy the
didactic impulse of a Chang Hui-yen. All these differences can

perhaps be reduced into two basic attitudes toward the writing of *tz'u*; Kung Tzu-chen writes *tz'u* as an expression of feeling; Chang Hui-yen, typical of the scholar-poets, regards poeticizing as an exercise of the intellect. Such being the case, T'an Hsien's grouping of poets in terms of "former and later" is again a revelation of the Ch'ing poets' preponderant concern with the question of tradition and model.

An inevitable question now arises: how useful and legitimate is the term "school" (*p'ai*)? Theoretical statements by a given group almost never tell the full story of a literary history; the Ch'ang-chou "school" has indeed proposed a very impressive critical theory, but this does not mean that all the Ch'ang-chou poets have actualized that ideal in their creative output. The Che-hsi "school" has been described as lacking in a comprehensive theory; yet it has certainly produced some superb poems. Let us cite an example by Li O:

> To the tune of "The Hundred-Word Ditty"
> —On a moonlit night, I passed by the Seven-Miles Rapids.[42] The sights were exceptionally enchanting. As I sang this tune, all the mountains seemed to resound [with my song]—

> The gleam of this autumn night
> Portrays for me, by the River T'ung,
> The noble legacy of bygone days.
> Such breezy, bedewed loveliness does not belong to the
>   human world;
> Alone, I sit at the prow and play my flute.
> The myriad sounds of nature arise from the mountains;
> A single star sparkles on the water:
> Perhaps this is the continuation of that dream about
>   the crane.[43]
> The creaking of oars subsides in the distance;
> At the western cliff, the fisherman has just retired.[44]

> My mind goes back to the group of Hsi-she[45]
>   long buried in history;
> Their lofty abandon has now faded away,
> Leaving me isolated.
> In perfect silence, a few cold fireflies
> Thread among the thatched huts at yonder bay.
> The woods, in their crystal stillness, hide the mist;
> The peaks, with their soaring precipices, check the moon;

> While a dark sail vacillates in the ethereal green of
>   land and sky.
> Drifting on with the currents,
> The white clouds return to the deep valleys
>   to sink into sleep.

Any translation into English cannot possibly do this poem justice. There are indeed some allusions; but the allusive words are so skillfully woven into the fabric of sensory details that they hardly ruffle the verbal surface of the poem. The mood of a lone flutist and the mood of a rustic landscape are the subject of many a poem before; rarely, however, do they blend into such a harmonious whole. Such a piece can only be the result of the union of language and sensitivity; never the product of creative guidelines. Li O himself has indicated that "poetic style is a necessity; but the idea of 'school' is unnecessary."[46]

If "school" is indeed an unnecessary critical crutch, then Kung Tzu-chen may be spared the imputation of multiple imitator; like his fellow Ch'ing poets, he too sets out to elevate the status of *tz'u*, not by way of theoretical affirmation, but by way of confirming it as the medium of the expression of *ch'ing*. He speaks as a many-voiced dreamer (man of *ch'ing*): sometimes he recounts the dream in vivid details; sometimes he seems to be unaware of the difference between fantasy and vision; sometimes he laments the loss of dreamland upon awakening/returning; sometimes he is deliberately reticent about the ultimate meaning of the dream.

As for tributes from his contemporaries, none is more eloquent than that of Tuan Yü-ts'ai, the poet's maternal grandfather: "They [Kung's *tz'u*] contain the same wondrous sights as snow in a silver bowl and an egret bathed in moonlight. Most people just dabble at this business; few can attain such heights."[47]

CHAPTER 6

Flowers Fall, Flowers Bloom: Kung's Heritage and Influence

I want to write verses which are simple and plain,
But each time I lift my brush, I lose control of
   my lucid, my keen feelings.
Let me cast off the name of madman and abandon all
   thoughts:
Absolute silence will be my teacher.
   —*Miscellaneous Poems Written in the Capital from
   Spring to Summer of the Year Chi-mao* (1819),
   [No. 14, K 442]

K UNG Tzu-chen wrote these lines at the age of twenty-eight. It is
   a self-examination far from plain and simple. Its confessional
tone and underlying thematic tension foreshadow the kind of poetry
which he was "cursed" to write for two more decades. And the
paradox of the poem—versification and silence as two forms of self-
expression—also reflects the tension-filled life of the poet.

The central tension in Kung's life was basically a conflict between
the public man and the private self, between intellect and sentiment. This conflict was in fact common to many traditional Chinese
men of letters, for in the social and cultural context of old China,
scholarship was hopelessly entwined with officialdom, and literary
endeavors were considered secondary to political fulfillments. Many
writers resolved this conflict either by succeeding in public life or by
developing a positive aesthetic philosophy;[1] Kung, however, remained to the end a dispensable "minor official" and a reluctant
poet, a man torn between two worlds. Whether Kung's is a unique
case, a coincidence of sensibility and circumstances, or just a typical

131

example of the poetic temperament of his time will have to be decided by further studies of Ch'ing poetry, especially that of the first half of the nineteenth century.

Nevertheless, Kung Tzu-chen's conflict abundantly enriched his poetry. The central tension in the poet's life is represented by a pair of recurrent images—the flute and the sword. Associated with the flute motif are: aesthetic life and the quiet south ("How many flute songs fill the southeast?"—p. 39); childhood innocence and maternal love ("The flute of the candy seller sobs in a narrow lane,/ . . . Then my mother knew I was ill . . . "—p. 45); reclusion and solitary enlightenment ("Outside of flute music in autumn lakes and hills,/ There is no place in this world without sorrow."—p. 40); and the mental turmoils of the night ("They leave a lingering flavor appropriate to the flute."—p. 40). Associated with the sword motif are: heroic deeds and the open frontier ("Whose icy sword guards the northwest?"—p. 39); zealous ideals and political ambition ("In my youth I wielded the sword and played the flute . . . "—p. 98); friendship and chivalrous generosity ("A lengthy memorial,/ A priceless sword,[2]/ Rarely come from the same person."—K 557); and practical concerns of the day ("They come in angry torrents and I must brandish my sword."—p. 39). The flute and sword are often juxtaposed in a larger metaphor in which poetry and sword-wielding represent variant ways for the poet to gratify a creative urge which "has been raging for a thousand years like tidal waves" (p. 39). In this metaphor, poetic creativity ("the spring of overflowing words which gushes out at night"—p. 41) is united with titanic ambition ("unsheathe our swords in a dream"—p. 40), both being the involuntary results of a fervent spirit in search of an adequate form of self-expression. Together these contrasting, interlocking motifs give Kung's poetry tight thematic structure and unusual intellectual richness.

Complementing Kung's imagistic antithesis of the flute and the sword is a wide range of diction and tone. On the whole, the poetic voice is split into that of the public scholar-critic and that of the private poet-lover. In his public verse, the tone is generally satiric, ranging from fanciful jest in the *Hsiao yu-hsien tz'u* ("Short Lyrics on Travels in the Immortals' Realm") to sardonic humor in the *yung-shih* poems (supposedly on "historical" events); examples of both have been discussed in Chapter Three. A great portion of these satiric verses are political allegories written in the long and free-flowing ancient verse form (*ku t'i*), whose narrative contents have correlated orders of meaning in the poet's life. The language of the public verses is almost without fail that of a masterful satirist and an egoistic scholar: acid, hyperbolic, and often deliberately difficult or obscure. The obscurity comes partly from what seems to be Kung's irreverent attitude toward his craft and his readers, and partly from his training in ancient literature and paleography. Arcane terms and enigmatic expressions often appear in breathless rhythmic passages spellbinding and bewildering the reader. Sometimes we get the impression that displaying his multifaceted learning in social satires is Kung's way of showing contempt for conventional values.

Beneath the exuberant and relentless social critic lies the private poet whose deep-seated longings and dreams are not bound by the social-historical context of any particular age. Kung's conflicting emotions are best dramatized by the sudden change of tone he uses to tell the story of his "flute-like heart." While Kung's satiric verses reflect the concerns and disappointments of an involved scholar-poet, his lyrical poetry, especially the *tz'u* lyrics and some of the quatrains, is basically a spontaneous expression of his private feelings and moods—private expressions which nevertheless have universality. Moods vary from tender nostalgia ("Suddenly I recall my peculiar child mind./ A red lamp glows through endless time."—p. 44) to quiet despair ("Planting flowers is planting the seeds of sorrow."—p. 53). In these lyrical reflections on the meaning and nature of human experience, external scenes tinted with subjectivity (e.g., "Countless huge stars glisten/ As the moon sinks across the long sky into the tree tops."—p. 39) and inner landscapes evoked from memory (e.g., "A certain river, a certain hill: your name lost;/ One hairpin, one pendant: your slightest trace also gone."—p. 65) replace the social settings and typed characters of the satiric verses. The diction of these personal poems, a delicate blend of the resonant language of conventional lyrics and Buddhist terms such as "penitence" and "meditation," also contrasts sharply with the exuberant style of Kung's public verses.

Between the public satire and the personal lyrics lies a group of poems similar in language and structure to the "Miscellaneous Poems No. 14" quoted at the beginning of this chapter. In these poems conflicts are stated directly instead of implied by imagistic tension or tonal contrast. Some of these poems bear the unmistakable imprint of Zen logic.

Such a multitude of styles and voices gives Kung Tzu-chen's poetry, upon first reading, a mosaic quality which confuses and dazzles at the same time. Kung's exuberance also makes the critical task of historical placement, particularly with respect to the problem of heritage and influence, an extremely difficult one. While Kung's own dictum that "I only start trends" has turned out, as we shall see later, to be prophetic, his relationship with earlier poets is still a question largely unanswered.[3] In fact, the question of historical assessment has divided Kung's readership into three groups. The first group finds his exuberance cloying and so dismisses both the poet and his work with epithets like "flippant" and "wayward style" (*wei t'i*).[4] A second group, however, perceives in the same exuberance a "refreshing departure" from hackneyed tradition and considers him to be one of the major innovators of Ch'ing poetry.[5] Still a third group seeks to affirm Kung's poetic stature within the tradition of Chinese poetry by linking him with many earlier masters, usually on impressionistic grounds. We shall now briefly examine some of the suggestions made by this third group; these suggestions occasionally go beyond the purely evaluative approach of the detractors and the enthusiasts, and often shed light on Kung's poetic style and inspiration.[6]

Kung Tzu-chen's style is said to have recaptured the spirit of Li Po; his love lyrics, the grace and passion of Li Shang-yin.[7] Besides echoing T'ang poetry, Kung's *shih* is said to bear the imprint of T'ao Ch'ien (365–427), Lu Yu (1125–1210), Wu Wei-yeh (1609–72), and the two pre-Han masterpieces, *Chuang tzu* and *Ch'u tz'u*.

Some of these suggestions seem valid and indeed illuminate certain aspects of Kung's *shih* style; but some are based on flimsy evidence. Of all the comparisons suggested, the one with T'ao Ch'ien is the least tenable: the sole justification for linking Kung and T'ao is a series of three quatrains in the Chi-hai medley (K 521–22) in which Kung pays homage to T'ao's noble character and laments the latter's involuntary reclusion.[8] T'ao Ch'ien, according to Kung, has been a much misunderstood poet; behind the facade of "serenity," the traditional characteristic attributed to T'ao, actually hides a man burning with ambitions, a man with the indomitable will of a Ching K'o and the heart of a Chu-ko Liang.[9] While Kung's unorthodox interpretation of T'ao Ch'ien the man is surely an extension of his own self-image—a poet longing to be a swordsman and an active participant in statesmanship—Kung's and T'ao's poetic

sensibilities are independent of each other. T'ao Ch'ien is remembered for his bucolic poetry and his immersion in rustic life.
Even in his reflective poems of Confucian sincerity and Taoist
quietude, T'ao's ideas are usually dressed in images from nature
(e.g., the homing birds, the "indomitable pine tree," the "unswept
paths").[10] Kung Tzu-chen, on the other hand, rarely writes about
the rustic side of nature or describes a scene objectively; his
reflections on experience are usually recorded in discursive language.

The suggestion that Lu Yu influenced Kung is based on two
observations: that three of Kung's *chüeh-chü* lines seem to be
borrowed from Lu, with only minor changes in wording; and that
both Kung and Lu use parallelism in their *chüeh-chü*.[11] Both observations are only partially correct, and neither can support the
suggestion of influence. While the borrowing of ideas and expressions commonly occurs in Chinese poetry, the contention that
Kung's parallelism reflects Lu's influence actually turns an exception into a rule: Kung employs parallel lines sparingly in his *chüeh-
chü* and shuns the decorative use of parallelism (see Chapter Four);
Lu Yu frequently used parallel structure in the *chüeh-chü*,
sometimes only to create a prosodic effect.[12] Besides his immaculate
attention to prosody, Lu also wrote two kinds of poetry which Kung
never touched upon: "patriotic" verse, filled with topical references
and martial expressions; and poems about life in the countryside,
characterized by graphic descriptions of rural landscape and the
simple activities of farm people.[13]

The argument in favor of Wu Wei-yeh's influence on Kung relies
on biographical and literary evidence. The biographical evidence is
found in Kung's three *chüeh-chü* on his three favorite Ch'ing poets,
one of whom is Wu Wei-yeh. The literary data consist of two poems,
one *yung-shih shih* (poetry on historical events) and one *ku-t'i shih*
(poetry in the ancient verse form), the latter a conscious imitation of
Wu's florid style.[14] The argument, again, is valid only superficially.
While Kung professes in the respective *chüeh-chü* his fondness for
the three Ch'ing poets, he also points out that their appeal to him is
inseparable from his fond memories of his mother. It was she who
introduced him to the world of poetry in general and the three
Ch'ing poets in particular; he returns to them in adulthood, then,
for sentimental reasons, "knowing very well that they are not the
best in literature."[15] The literary evidence has little substance as

well. Since one of the two poems in question is a deliberate emula-
tion of Wu's style, it cannot really be cited as an example of stylistic
resemblance. The other poem, a lampoon of the pathetic behavior of
the Ch'ing literati living under the prevailing fear of literary in-
quisitions (p. 59), warrants a closer look. The poem is said to be
"extremely" reminiscent of Wu Wei-yeh's characteristic style,[16]
probably on account of its smooth rhythm and its relatively
transparent language. The analogy, however, is valid only to a limited extent, and does not apply to Kung and Wu's poetry as a whole.
Wu Wei-yeh's distinction lies in his long historical narratives (ko-
hsing), generally marked by a prevailing mood of sorrow and nostalgia, and a touch of light irony in the portrayal of central characters; Kung's historical narratives are basically allegories brimming
with indignation over the abuses and follies of a whole stratum of
society. In their handling of language, too, the two poets are far
apart. Kung sprinkles his historical satires with harsh and arcane
words to create a rugged rhythm and an archaic flavor, not so much
to persuade as to startle and shock unwary readers. Wu Wei-yeh, on
the other hand, builds up a unified mood in a rambling narrative
with polished diction and a melodious prosody: it is a style, as one
critic has observed, "full of nuances and coquettish charms; the one
thing it lacks is an archaic flavor."[17]

So far, the contentions of influence on Kung's style are limited to
particular features of his poetry. The suggestions of T'ang dynasty
inspiration, however, get closer to Kung's creative secrets. Unfortunately, most of the suggestions come in the form of general
statements; for example, Kung's love lyrics are said to be reminiscent of Li Shang-yin, and his overall style a direct descendant of Li
Po. Further investigation of these claims is necessary to understand
Kung's position in Chinese poetry.

That Kung Tzu-chen recalls Li Shang-yin is to a certain extent
supportable. In diction, imagery, and the use of allusions, the two
poets sometimes echo each other, especially in their elegant seven-
character lines: both wrote wistful lyrics with ornate diction and
paired images such as *luan* and *feng* (female and male phoenixes);[18]
both make use of similar allusions, the most notable of which is the
story of Tung-fang So and the peaches of immortality;[19] both set
their allegorical poems in fairyland or mythological places, although
for different purposes: Li Shang-yin conceals an ambiguous love
affair or suggests hopeless passion with mythological archetypes;[20]

Kung Tzu-chen, on the other hand, uses the language—for example, The Milky Way, a red wall, fairy maidens—and the common devices of mythology, such as the celestial journey, primarily to build a dramatic structure for his social satires. For instance, Kung's fifteen "Short Lyrics on Travels in the Immortals' Realm" are self-contained episodes linked together by the journey device.

However, these occasional similarities of diction and narrative technique should not obscure the fundamental difference between the two poets. Each approaches the poetic problems of imagery differently. Li Shang-yin's poems are fraught with an imagery which ranges from common figures (e.g., "winged guest" for the gathering bee) to highly ingenious puns and conceits; for example, in his famous line "The spring silkworm's thread will only end when death comes,"[21] the futility of passion is objectified in physical terms, and *ssu*/silk is a subtle pun on *ssu*/lovesickness.[22] Kung Tzu-chen's lyrics, particularly those on love and autumnal moods, seldom involve violent conceits; rather, they express tender sorrows through a flow of lilting sounds (e.g., "In a wind full of fallen petals I leave the south."—p. 40). Li's is a visual imagination; Kung's is basically rhetorical.

The casual reader is likely to overlook a fundamental difference in the creative attitudes of the two poets. Li Shang-yin is a consummate artist who invests his love poems with a subtle irony;[23] for example, is his well-known couplet "Is Ch'ang O sorry that she stole the magic herb?/ Between the blue sky and the emerald sea, thinking night after night?"[24] to be read literally or ironically? We cannot be certain whether Li writes with genuine compassion for the futility of human choice,[25] or whether, as some critics have suggested, he merely uses an ingenious conceit to chide the faithlessness of a Taoist nun, his former lover, by comparing her solitude in the convent to that of the ill-fated moon-goddess.[26] Kung's love lyrics, however, are often tinged with romantic intensity and religious insight. His is not a conscious artistry, but an expression of intuitive knowledge. Lines such as "If by chance the Zen barrier is smashed—/A person beautiful as jade, a sword like a rainbow" (p. 55) mark a visible departure from both the simple lyricism of the seventh and the eighth centuries, and the verbal sophistication of the Late T'ang.

Kung's kinship with Li Shang-yin is basically limited to their treatment of the seven-character *chin-t'i* form (quatrains and eight-line regulated verse), but his relationship with Li Po is of a much broader nature. Even a casual reading of Kung's "Song of Rejuvenation" (K 452–53) and Li's "The Szechwan Road" (*Shu-tao nan*) reveals striking similarities: a hyperbolic and highly alliterative language; a predilection for grandiloquence; and a delightfully imaginative handling of mood and scene. (Kung's is an ecstatic account of his life and wishes, while Li's is a rhapsodic description of wild landscape.)[27] Kung's "A Song on the Fallen Petals in West Country" (p. 62) and Li's acclaimed "Song before Drinking" *(Chiang chin chiu)* are two other superb examples of how exuberant moods can be sustained with rhapsodic rhythm and intoxicating language.[28] However, Li and Kung are most strongly linked by their concern with the swordsman ideal. Li Po, like Kung, wrote about the sorrow of an unused sword, the despair of a circling phoenix which yearns for, but cannot find, a worthy tree in which to settle.[29]

The sword image goes directly to the heart of Kung's poetic inspiration; the image of the unused sword and its concomitant frustration are recurrent motifs in Chinese poetry, motifs binding not only Kung Tzu-chen and Li Po, but a host of other kindred spirits as well. Other resemblances between these poets are only superficial and always arguable; for example, in his tumbling songs, Kung's style resembles Li Po's most, but his work lacks the ecstatic response to wild nature characteristic of Li Po. Li Po paints part of the rugged landscape of eighth-century China, frequently with a sublime imagination; Kung Tzu-chen, the possessor of a highly civilized sensibility, sketches a landscape not with actual observations of the physical world, but with literary and mythological allusions. Yet, despite the changes of poetic responses to nature, the sword image remains.

Kung Tzu-chen's literary indebtedness extends to the influential *Chuang tzu* and *Ch'u tz'u*.[30] This influence actually is not a critical discovery; Kung suggested it himself on several occasions. In a laudatory passage on Li Po's character and career, Kung comments on Li's cultural and literary heritage: "Chuang-tzu and Ch'ü Yüan are two incompatible types [of sensibility]; the union of the two as a way of feeling begins with Li. Confucians, Taoist Immortals, and wandering knights represent three incompatible types [of ideals]; the union of the three in one temperament also begins with Li."[31] His encomium is in praise not only of Li but also of himself, for Kung evidently sees himself as heir to the same cultural forces:

An unusual dream born of profound truth,
A spring heart chiseled in beautiful words—
The two tenacious ghosts of Chuang and Ch'ü
Have taken hold of my inside, deep and unyielding.
Since time immemorial they may not be possessed together;
How could I bear both of them in the square inch of
    my heart?   [K 485]

The "unusual dream" in the first line refers to the famous dream
recorded in the *Ch'i-wu lun* chapter of the *Chuang tzu*, in which the
legendary philosopher undergoes transfiguration and experiences
the joy of a carefree butterfly. The "spring heart" of the second line
alludes to the "Summons of the Soul" (*Chao hun*) in the *Ch'u tz'u*
which concludes with: "Infinite sights of a thousand miles grieve my
heart of spring./ Come back, oh soul; full of sorrow is the southern
land." Behind the mournful language, lies, of course, the Ch'ü Yüan
legend and its moral which, as understood and propagated by the
literary men of China, is loyalty to the land and political involvement at all costs.[32] The two "tenacious ghosts" which Kung has to
wrestle with are, therefore, the intellectual detachment of a
Chuang-tzu as symbolized by the butterfly dream, and the emotional anguish of a Ch'ü Yüan, vividly recorded in the *Ch'u tz'u*. In
his effort to reconcile the contentious "ghosts" within himself, Kung
Tzu-chen not only paraphrases a perennial conflict in the Chinese
literary temperament, but also provides a clue to the recurrence of
the sword image.

The sword image is actually a dichotomous figure: the unused
sword registers the anguish of unrecognized or rejected talent; the
active sword romanticizes knight-errantry and its attendant heroic
ideals and unconventional values.[33] The sword can thus be an image
of despair, an extension of the keynote of the Ch'ü Yüan myth, or
one of exultation, capturing the spirit of the *Chuang tzu*, especially
by affirming the freedom of the individual. The metaphorical
"sword" is seldom used in one sense exclusively. And it appears
most often in the type of poetry which is marked by a stress on the
poet's "personality."

Kung Tzu-chen and Li Po use the sword primarily as a symbol of
exultation—a way of transcending sorrow and frustration; there are
other poets, however, who emphasize its melancholic side. Recent
studies of the T'ang poet Li Ho, for instance, have revealed a

complex personality which challenges the stereotyped image of the Chinese poet as either an ineffectual aesthete who reconciles his failure in a bureaucratic society with wine and versification, or a statesman-aesthete who seeks truths in eternal nature. Li Ho, the bureaucratic failure,[34] has emerged from critical scrutiny as a "modern" figure torn between worldly ambitions, social conscience, and sensual delights on the one hand, and an intense desire for intuitive knowledge and spiritual liberation on the other.[35] The torment of this personality is manifested in a poetic language which comprises bare, acid lines of social protest as well as exotic subjects and fantastic imagery. The same poet who painstakingly describes the nuances of elementary nature, a nature often seen in a hallucinatory light, also writes: "Seeking a style, culling my phrases,/ Grown old carving grubs!"[36] One of the consistent images in Li Ho's poetry is also the sword, an unused sword "hidden in a case."

The sword also appears as a significant image in the poetry of T'ao Ch'ien, the "recluse-poet," a fact which Kung Tzu-chen pointed out emphatically in his three quatrains on T'ao. T'ao Ch'ien is the pastoral poet par excellence who has been idolized throughout Chinese poetry as a man of detachment and "serenity" (p'ing tan); however, T'ao's alleged contempt for "empty fame" (hsü ming) and his rejection of the bureaucratic life are belied by personal ambition hidden in his poetry: his repeated identification with Ch'ü Yüan and his glowing tributes to some of the monumental swordsmen in Chinese history.[37]

The foregoing comparisons are not meant to suggest that Kung Tzu-chen, Li Po, and Li Ho all wrote the same kind of poetry; for despite their common "sword"—their common burden—each poet had his own "flute," his own music. The comparisons do suggest, however, that the perennial issue of the poet's divided loyalty—to the state and to the self—gave rise to a recurrent motif embodied in the sword image; and that the sword imagery bears the twin inspirations of the Chuang tzu and the Ch'u tz'u.

Kung Tzu-chen is also indebted to the Chuang tzu and the Ch'u tz'u for his variegated language and his unique rhetoric. The influence of the Chuang tzu is noticeable in the hyperbolic language, the rolling rhythms, and the playful tone of Kung's long songs (hence, the impression of Kung's resemblance to Li Po, who was also inspired by the style of the Chuang tzu). The influence of the Ch'u tz'u is more pervasive and is not restricted to any particular verse form. Kung's political allegories are clearly inspired by the symbolism of the *Li sao*, or "Encountering Sorrow"; part of his *chüeh-chü* diction comes from the exotic language of the *Chao hun*, or "Summons of the Soul." However, Kung Tzu-chen captures the mood and flavor of the *Ch'u tz'u* language most successfully in his personal lyrics, particularly those bitter-sweet lines about the "autumn soul" which departs from the southern landscape and the "flute songs" which linger in the limpid southern air. In these lines, two millennia of Chinese lyricism has come full circle.

It is Kung Tzu-chen's accomplishment that he revitalized the sword motif, the public burden of the literary man, without sacrificing the lyricism of the *Ch'u tz'u*. This is his fundamental indebtedness to his literary forebears; this is also his legacy to his poetic heirs. When he died in 1841, the Opium War, which shocked China into manifold reforms and eventual revolution, had already begun; a new breed of poets, bursting with ambition and enthusiasm for a "new dawn," were on the way. These newcomers were both the reformers of late Ch'ing and the "revolutionary" poets of the early Republic era. Through them, Kung Tzu-chen redeemed his prophecy that he was a "starter of trends."

In the century following Kung's death, Chinese poetry, like any other cultural realm, was dominated by a restless spirit and a strong desire for change and emancipation. The general trend toward the liberation of prosodic rules and creative attitudes resulted in an overall eclecticism in diction, style, and subject matter. Despite the "twilight struggle" of the traditionalists, the classical norms—ornate diction, meticulous prosody, and restrained mood—gradually gave way to a new poetry characterized by semi-vernacular language, multifarious interests, and an increasing cosmopolitanism.[38]

The first phase of this "progressive" trend culminated in the works of Huang Tsun-hsien (1848–1905) who advocated the refurbishing of old verse forms with new themes and a flexible linguistic medium. ("My hand writes what my mouth says."[39]) The second phase began with an earnest search for literary inspirations from the West which brought to China nineteenth-century "Romantic" notions such as democratic individualism, the mystery of love, and nationalism. However, mutation is seldom the law of literary history. Throughout this liberalizing trend—particularly between the two phases—those poets who had not been thoroughly "Westernized" still looked to their own native tradition for creative guides; and in Kung Tzu-chen they found a link between the old and the new.[40] Kung Tzu-chen's search for inner truths and his expressed concern over the fate of the nation accorded well with the sentiment of the age. His supple language, in particular, appealed to the transitional poets, who needed a similarly workable medium to express the lyrical side of their personalities. (The vernacular language did not become a mature poetic medium until the 1920s.[41]) Huang-Tsun-hsien, the "reformer of poetry," for instance, used colloquialism and even dialecticisms in his folk songs and many war chronicles, but chose a more refined language to convey his reflective moods. Many of Huang's seven-character *chüeh-chü* are said to have been inspired by Kung Tzu-chen;[42] and a critic has observed with nostalgia that the seven-character quatrains of Kung and Huang represent the "sunset glow" of a fine tradition.[43]

However, Kung Tzu-chen's most vocal enthusiasts were the political reformers and visionary spirits active at the turn of the twentieth century. The reasons for their support are not hard to understand. In the first place, Kung's dual concern with the "salvation" of both the state and the private self matched the emotional needs of the radical intellectuals at that time: Kung's "sword" symbolized their own desire for action; his "flute" comforted their fervent and eventually disillusioned souls. Ironically, the emotional hysteria of these activists had been anticipated by Kung Tzu-chen in a poem on the fate of the scholars of late Ming:

> Before they could establish themselves, the empire
>   had changed.
> Half of them became martyrs, half of them monks. [K 451]

Some of the Ch'ing reformers and revolutionaries did become martyrs; and one of them literally a monk. Their frustrated objective, however, was not to defend a native dynasty against alien rule, but to revitalize an alien dynasty through reform or to overthrow it. A second reason that these reformers and revolutionary poets eulogized Kung was that most of them were from the south and southeast, Kung Tzu-chen's home-country. Kung's particular concern over the welfare of the south and his frequent references to the southern landscape had a sentimental appeal to these southerners. Kung's popularity among the activist-intellectuals at the turn of the century has been well documented.[44] Here is an eye-witness's account by Wu Mi (1894–):

The poetry of [Kung] Ting-an is refreshingly novel in ideas and style; it has explored and exposed many new territories. I myself think that his poetry was the beacon of the reform movement; for a change in political trends is more often than not signaled by a change in literary trends. . . . Some, however, have slighted Ting-an's works because of its alleged lack of grace and seriousness. A consensus has to wait till later times. Let us now look at his influence. Ting-an's poetry has been extremely popular since the middle years of the Kuang-hsü era [1874–1908]. Before the year Keng-tzu [1900], when I was still a child, every household of the professed new-party members [i.e., the reformers] I visited had a copy of Ting-an's poems on the desk. Poets, too, vied with one another in imitating his style; for instance, even a master-poet like Liang Jen-kung [Ch'i-ch'ao] modeled . . . lines after Ting-an's. . . . In those days, there was also a vogue for assembling Ting-an's lines into new poems [*chi chü*] to circulate among one another. Of late, this practice has especially been indulged in by the Nan-she [Southern Society] poets. . . .[45]

Thus Kung Tzu-chen has touched three generations of poets: the poetic innovators of the second half of the nineteenth century, among them Huang Tsun-hsien; the political reformers of late Ch'ing, such as Liang Ch'i-ch'ao; and a group of younger men who considered themselves "revolutionaries" but did not become literarily active until after the Revolution of 1911—the Nan-she or Southern Society poets.[46] Kung's impact on these three generations varied according to each's literary temper and needs. To the reformers of poetics, Kung's daring departure from some of the woeful practices of Ch'ing poetry—affected mannerisms, stale sentiments, and slavish imitation of T'ang and Sung models—paved the road for subsequent formal and linguistic innovations, most of which persisted into the twentieth century. To the political reformers, some of whom were also advocates of a "poetic revolution" as part of a sweeping program to rejuvenate China's "spiritless" culture, Kung's social consciousness and spontaneity seemed to authenticate their own reformist zeal in politics and art.[47] Many leaders of the ill-fated Hundred Days Reforms of 1898, K'ang Yu-wei (1858–1927) in particular, not only read Kung Tzu-chen avidly but also turned to him for verbal borrowings; consequently, their own lines often echo Kung's in phrasing and ideas, especially those reflecting on social ills and the pervasive disillusionment of idealists.[48] Although only poets by avocation (as most of China's traditional men of letters were), these Ch'ing reformers nevertheless contributed to Chinese poetry by restoring the emotionalism which typified the *Ch'u tz'u*, an emotionalism which had been recently revitalized by Kung Tzu'chen's relentless attacks on Ch'ing institutions and his anguish over his failure to reconcile the roles of public man and private artist. The younger "revolutionaries" of the Southern Society brought this emotionalism into the twentieth century.

The Southern Society, a large literary association with a strong interest in national affairs (the founding members were all professed "revolutionaries"), flourished during the 1910s and 1920s. Its membership was eclectic and comprised some of the most prominent public figures and a varied group of intellectuals; there were, for example, participants of the 1911 Revolution and even a "romantic" monk. Besides their public concerns and activities, most members were inclined to express their variegated moods in "traditional" poetry, often in language quoted verbatim from Kung Tzu-chen.[49] It has been calculated that no less than 1588 lines of the "assembled verses," or *chi chü*, written by members of the Southern Society were borrowed from Kung; 73% of these lines, in fact, were taken from the Chi-hai quatrains.[50] Most of the Chi-hai lines they quoted pertained to three themes: the sorrow of an ineffectual scholar (*shu sheng*) living in a portentous age; nostalgia for the passing of youth and ambition; and the tenderness of love.

That the Chi-hai quatrains should have a particular appeal to these early Republican poets is not hard to understand. Like Kung Tzu-chen on his way "home," these young intellectuals were basically disillusioned idealists undertaking in their writings an emotional journey of adjustment. However, by the time their literary activity was under way, the emotional focus of their idealism, the 1911 Revolution, had ended, leaving in its wake a shattered country and many shattered dreams. The Revolution only triggered continual power struggles and numerous "corrective" wars among the rising military strongmen; the era of unification and democracy, which the Revolution had promised, remained a dream, for the country was blighted as ever. The idealists of the revolutionary era became a group of ineffectual men of letters living in a society run by the mechanism of political intrigue and military violence. Part of their reaction to this bleak age was a steady retreat into the private worlds of friendship, love, and religious consolation. What followed was a new surge of lyricism in classical poetry. Of the Southern Society poets, the one who came closest to recapturing the wistful mood of the Chi-hai quatrains was the monk (Su) Man-shu (1884–1918):

Miscellaneous Poems while Living in Japan [No. 10]

Lamplight against a pearl screen, jade harp singing
  of autumn—
Winding balustrades curve about the lakeside tower.
Suddenly I recall Ting-an's plaintive line:
"For three lives I have dreamed of Soochow, florid
  and foliant."

. . . . .

At Wu Men (Soochow), to the Rhymes of Scholar I [No. 11]

White water, green hills, lingering thoughts—
Everywhere from heaven to earth a drizzly mist.
Light wind, fine rain, a red clay monastery—
The swallows are returning, but not the monk.

Although the landscape in these lines has appeared in the Chi-hai quatrains before (see pp. 86 and 93), the tone is a trifle too soft for Kung Tzu-chen. Man-shu, the translator of Byron and Shelley, actually fuses in these lines the cadence of classical language and the sentiments of a self-styled modern "Romantic." His "unreturning" monk is he himself: Man-shu, the cosmopolitan poet-revolutionary who wandered perpetually in search of novel experiences. With Man-shu the romantic monk began a new phase of Chinese lyricism. When the Southern Society faded out in the mid-twenties, the literature of China had already taken on a "modern" look after a whole decade of experimentation with the vernacular language (*pai-hua*) and Western forms and ideas. Several years later, a group of new poets were to continue Man-shu's search for "truth and beauty," although theirs was to be a "plainer" language.

Classical poetry, however, did not die with the emergence of the new poetry. Some "old" sentiments still appeared in the compact *chüeh-chü* form, and sometimes came from unexpected quarters. In the summer of 1933, a calamitous event which shocked literary circles throughout China took place in Shanghai: the assassination of Yang Ch'üan (1893–1933), a prominent economist, an active participant in the 1911 Revolution, and a former member of the Southern Society.[51] Yang's death was attributed to his involvement with the Chinese Alliance for the Protection of Human Rights (*Chung-kuo min-ch'üan pao-chang t'ung-meng*), an organization formed by a group of progressive intellectuals to counteract government censorship and harsh measures against nonconformist writers. One of Yang's outraged friends was Lu Hsün (1881–1936), essayist, relentless social critic, doyen of modern literature, and an active member of the same organization. Yang's funeral was held on a rainy day; Lu Hsün, noted for his acid style and intellectual arrogance, elegized his fallen comrade in a mournful *chüeh-chü*, the exact verse form of the Chi-hai quatrains. Its flowing rhythm and understated sorrow prompted a close associate to say that it was "practically a replica of Kung Tzu-chen."[52]

Lament for Yang Ch'üan

> Where are the flowing feelings of yesterday?
> Flowers bloom, flowers fall; such is the course of
>   things.
> Who could have foreseen these tears in a southern rain,
> Mourning once more the passing of a gallant son?

Lu Hsün's poem brings back memories of a tormented Ch'ü Yüan lamenting the departure of a compatriot soul. In this personal tribute to a southern martyr, the funerary sorrow of a whole class of scholar-poets who wrote and acted under the burden of public conscience converges. The swordsman ideal which links Kung Tzu-chen to his poetic forebears returns once again in the "gallant son" whom Lu Hsün mourns, although by Lu Hsün's time a whole century of momentous changes had already pushed China brusquely onto the modern stage and propelled Chinese literature into a new era. The swordsman is a "tenacious ghost"; he will be around as long as poets choose to write both as private dreamers and men of social commitment. And only such poets can remain part of their historical milieu without sacrificing the universality which is the special property of poetic language. Kung Tzu-chen is one such poet. His sword motif recurs in Chinese poetry and clearly belongs to the public; but his flute songs are uniquely his own.

Notes and References

Chapter One

1. Wang T'ung (583–616) of the Sui dynasty taught near the confluence of the Yellow River and the Fen River. Fang Hsüan-ling (578–648) and Tu Ju-hui (died A.D. 630), who became renowned prime ministers of the T'ang dynasty, were supposed to be among Wang's disciples. Since the time of Ssu-ma Kuang (1019–86) of the Sung dynasty, many scholars have come to doubt this on the ground that if there really had been a Wang T'ung with disciples as famous as Fang and Tu, such a person would not have been neglected by the historical records, expecially the Sui dynastic history; see Tanaka Kenji's commentaries in *Kyo Ji-chin (Chugoku shijin senshū*, ser. 2, vol. XIV; Tokyo, 1962), pp. 141–42, and the commentaries in *Chin-tai shih-hsüan* (Peking, 1963), pp. 37–38. Kung Tzu-chen's own note to this poem reads: "I have never had a disciple in my life." See *Kung Tzu-chen ch'üan-chi* (2 vols.; Shanghai: Chung Hua, 1959), p. 519; this is the edition of Kung's collected works used in this book and hereafter will be referred to simply as K, followed by the page number.

2. For an account of the literary inquisition, see L. C. Goodrich, *The Literary Inquisition of Ch'ien-lung* (Baltimore: Waverly Press, 1935). The translation of the entire poem referred to here can be found in Chapter Four, section VI.

3. Kung's insistence on applying scholarship to practical issues and matters of government is in the tradition of the so-called New Text School of interpreting the Six Classics. This school, dated from the Former Han, concentrated on elucidating the "esoteric dicta and great dogma" (*wei-yen ta-i*) of the Kung-yang commentary to the *Spring and Autumn Annals*, where political implications abound. (The above rendition of the term *wei-yen ta-i* is taken from Professor Hsiao Kung-ch'üan's article, "K'ang Yu-wei and Confucianism," *Monumenta Serica*, XVIII [1959]: 96–212.) As can be seen from No. 59 of the *Miscellaneous Poems of the Year Chi-hai* [K 514] and the "Song on the Talents of Ch'ang-chou" [K 494–59], Kung Tzu-chen had been a student of Liu Feng-lu (1776–1829); furthermore, many of Kung's friends belonged to the Ch'ang-chou School, which revived the New Text tradition in Ch'ing times. However, as is typical of him, Kung never

rigidly followed the tenets of any school. Thus, we find him also praising masters of the Old Text tradition which, among other things, concentrated on verifying the individual words rather than examining the general meaning and application of a text. The following poem on Ma Yung of the Eastern or Later Han is such an example. The "K'ung wall" refers to a wall in the residence of Confucius in which was found the Old Text version of the *Book of History*. Here Kung is alluding to the Old Text Classics in general. According to his biography in the *Hou Han shu*, or *Dynastic History of the Later Han*, Ma was not too strict in his observance of Confucian decorum and conducted his classes in front of a red silk curtain, behind which music was played. Professor Hsiao informs me that this explains why Ma did not occupy a place in the Confucian Temple and also suggests one reason why Kung had such high regard for him.

Miscellaneous Poems of the Year Chi-hai [No. 56]

The tradition preserved by the K'ung wall
    was dim and dying
When he revived it before a red silk curtain
    to the accompaniment of music and songs.
Now that the texts of the Eastern Han have all
    been determined,
Why is there no place for Ma Yung in the Temple
    of Confucius?   [K 514]

Nor did Kung subscribe to the dogmatic division between the Han School of textual criticism and the Sung School of philosophical speculation, as can be seen from the following letter to Chiang Fan (1761–1831), an ardent exponent of the Han School:

I have finished reading your masterpiece. There are ten reasons why I am not comfortable with its title, *The Lineage of the Han School in This Dynasty.* I would change it to *The Lineage of Classical Learning in This Dynasty.* . . . If one considers the Han School and the Sung School as opponents, it will be even more unenlightened. Did not the people of Han times discuss human nature and the way of Heaven as well? . . . Did not the people of Sung times discuss factual findings as well? . . . The present dynasty in particular has unusual scholars who deal with texts that have no commentaries and make original discoveries in the Classics which do not belong to either the Han or the Sung school, but which endeavor only to find the truth . . . [K 347]

From this, it can be seen that Kung's association with the Ch'ang-chou School was due primarily to his enthusiasm for the practical application of scholarship rather than for any particular academic principle.

    4. Liang Ch'i-ch'ao, *Ch'ing-tai hsüeh-shu kai-lun* (Hong Kong, 1963), p. 54. This book has been translated by Immanuel C. Y. Hsü as *Intellectual*

Trends in the Ch'ing Period (Cambridge: Harvard University Press, 1959). The translation here is my own.

5. The period from the late eighteenth to the early nineteenth century represents a gap in scholarly research on the Ch'ing dynasty; many studies focus only on events after the Opium War. This lack of information has been pointed out by Wolfram Eberhard in *A History of China* (Berkeley and Los Angeles: University of California Press, 1969), p. 273. For example, the Ch'ien-lung Emperor's famous foreign wars are discredited by Eberhard as a possible cause of dynastic decline on the ground that, though expensive, they should not have been beyond the resources available to China at that time.

6. Hsiao I-shan, *Ch'ing-tai t'ung-shih* (Shanghai, 1928), II: 247.

7. Quoted in Ch'ien Mu, *Kuo-shih ta-kang* (Taipei, 1953), II: 625. Chang Hsüeh-ch'eng had traveled widely and seen much of the official corruption of his time; see Goodrich, *op. cit.*, p. 11. For an account of Chang's influence on Kung, especially regarding his views of the Six Classics and history, see David. S. Nivison, *The Life and Thought of Chang Hsüeh-ch'eng* (Stanford: Stanford University Press, 1966), pp. 281–82; Ch'ien Mu, *Chung-kuo chin san-pai-nien hsüeh-shu shih* (Taipei, 1957), pp. 535–36, 544–45; and Hou Wai-lu, *Chin-tai chung-kuo ssu-hsiang hsüeh-shuo shih* (Shanghai, 1947), p. 625.

8. Present-day scholars have, by and large, discredited the opium trade as the primary factor in the copper-silver exchange rate; see Arthur Waley, *The Opium War Through Chinese Eyes* (London: George Allen & Unwin, 1958), p. 25; Hsin-pao Chang, *Commissioner Lin and the Opium War* (Cambridge: Harvard University Press, 1964), p. 46; and Frank H. H. King, *Money and Monetary Policy in China, 1845–1895* (Cambridge: Harvard University Press, 1965), pp. 140–43.

9. "Green Coin" translates *ch'ing ch'ien*, the bronze coin of Ch'ing times which contained mostly copper and zinc, with a small percentage of lead and tin; see Lien-sheng Yang, *Money and Credit in China* (Cambridge: Harvard University Press, 1952), p. 37.

10. "Pint" translates *sheng*, a measure equivalent to 31.6 cubic inches. "Peck" translates *tou*, which is equal to ten *sheng*. Here, Kung refers to the many additional charges the people had to pay so that a state tax of three pints would amount to a whole peck. Consequently, the poet thought it might be better for the farmer to slaughter his ox than to raise crops and cope with taxation.

11. Cf., for instance, Eberhard, *op. cit.*, pp. 273–75; L. C. Goodrich, *A Short History of the Chinese People* (New York and Evanston: Harper & Row, 1963), p. 219, n. 4; and Ping-ti Ho, *Studies on the Population of China, 1368–1953* (Cambridge: Harvard University Press, 1959), p. 64.

12. Hung Liang-chi, "Essay on Livelihood" (*Sheng-chi p'ien*), quoted in Ch'ien Mu, *Kuo-shih ta-kang*, II: 626–27. Hung is sometimes known as "the Chinese Malthus"; see Ping-ti Ho, *op. cit.*, p. 271.

13. For an account of the 1774 uprising in Shantung, see Hsiao I-shan, *op. cit.*, II: 223–26.

14. Ch'ien Mu, *Kuo-shih ta-kang*, II: 627.

15. Eberhard, *op. cit.*, pp. 284–85. For a detailed account of the White Lotus Society, see Hsiao I-shan, *op. cit.*, II: 273–99.

16. Frederick Wakeman, Jr., "High Ch'ing: 1683–1839," *Modern East Asia: Essays in Interpretation*, ed. James B. Crowley (New York: Harcourt, Brace & World, 1970), p. 26.

17. For the career of Kung's father and grandfather, see Kung's chronological biography (*nien-p'u*) by Wu Ch'ang-shou appended in K 589 ff., or A. W. Hummel, *Eminent Chinese of the Ch'ing Period* (Washington: Government Printing Office, 1943–44), I: 431.

18. For a study of the so-called vertical rule of the Ch'ing emperors, see Wakeman, *op. cit.*, pp. 9–22.

19. For example, the well-known practice of kneeling three times and kotowing nine times (*san-kuei chiu-k'ou*) was initiated by the Ch'ing court. See Ch'ien Mu, *Kuo-shih ta-kang*, II: 599.

20. K 31.

21. K 36.

22. According to Chung-li Chang, *The Chinese Gentry* (Seattle and London: University of Washington Press, 1967), p. 121, the average age of the *chin-shih* graduates before the T'ai-p'ing period was 36. Therefore, for Kung to pass the metropolitan examinations at 38 was not such a late age as, for example, Tanaka, *op. cit.*, Preface, p. 22, has suggested.

23. Table 27 in Chung-li Chang, *op. cit.*, shows that in 1829, a total of 221 candidates made the grade of *chin-shih*; out of these, 54 were admitted to the Han-lin Academy. For further explanation of the metropolitan examinations, see *ibid.*, pp. 26–27; for a description of the content of these examinations and the emphasis on calligraphy, see *ibid.*, pp. 174–77. A brief account of the three ranks of *chin-shih* and the posts they were appointed to can be found in E-tu Zen Sun, *Ch'ing Administrative Terms* (Cambridge: Harvard University Press, 1961), pp. 200–2.

24. K 237–38.

25. K 105–11. A passage from this essay by Kung is translated in Ping-ti Ho, *op. cit.*, p. 273, as testimony to the alarming population increase at that time.

26. Hummel, *op. cit.*, I: 432.

27. Actually, Kung wrote these suggestions in the last year of the reign of Chia-ch'ing.

28. Quoted in Wu Ch'ang-shou's chronological biography of Kung in K 604.

29. Ch'ien Mu, *Kuo-shih ta-kang*, II: 618.

30. Hsiao I-shan, *op. cit.*, II: 46–47.

31. Chung-li Chang, *op. cit.*, p. 123.

32. According to a footnote in the Kuo-hsüeh fu-lun she edition of *Kung Ting-an ch'üan-chi (wen-chi*, II: 9a), the essay "Suggestions on Barring Foreign Ships from the Southeast" was concealed by Kung's son, Kung Ch'eng. This was probably due to the unpopularity of advocating the prohibition of foreign trade during the T'ung-chih and Kuang-hsü reigns. Kung Ch'eng, moreover, was associated with the British delegation and was said to have accompanied British troops in 1860 at the burning of the Yüan-ming Garden in Peking; see Hummel, *op. cit.,* I: 433; Ch'iu Yü-lin, *Ch'ing-tai i-wen* (Shanghai, 1932), *chüan* 5, pp. 30–31; and Wang T'ao, *Sung-pin so-hua* (Shanghai, 1934), *chüan* 5, p. 83.

33. K 169–71. For a more detailed account in English of Kung's suggestions and Lin's reply, see Hsin-pao Chang, *op. cit.,* pp. 126–28.

34. *Ibid.,* p. 212.

35. K 7.

36. According to Wu Ch'ang-shou, in K 600.

37. K 78.

38. As Kung indicated in one of his Chi-hai poems: "In my youth I wrote a masterpiece revering the recluse," K 532.

39. "Grand Secretariat" translates *luan-p'o*, which usually refers to the Han-lin Academy. Since Kung was not appointed to the Academy due to his unacceptable calligraphy, he might be using the term to refer to an institution close to it and at which he had served.

40. "The jade bridle-bells kept me company" alludes to Tu Fu's line: "Because of a breeze, I think of the jade bridle-bells" in a poem about staying overnight at the Censorate waiting to present a memorial (*Ch'un su tso-sheng*). Ancient officials rode to the morning audience on horseback. Kung is using this allusion to refer to his working into the night.

41. K 354.

42. For example, Chu Chieh-ch'in, *Kung Ting-an yen-chiu* (Taipei reprint, 1966), p. 10, mentions a Japanese writer who went so far as to claim that Kung would rather let China be divided by the Westerners than hand it over to the Manchus. Chu himself entitles one of his chapters "The Revolutionary Thoughts (*ko-ming ssu-hsiang*) of Kung Ting-an," although he interprets the term "revolution" in a broad sense. Hou Wai-lu, *op. cit.,* p. 628, however, specifically describes Kung's thoughts as bearing the seed of a "racial revolution" (*chung-tsu ko-ming*) and sees in Kung's writings a refusal to cooperate with the Ch'ing dynasty.

43. K 132–33.

44. Ch'iu Yü-lin, *op. cit.,* *chüan* 5, pp. 52–53.

45. Wei Chi-tzu, *Yü-ling shan-min i-shih*, p. 1b, in *Ku-hsüeh hui-k'an*, vol. XIII.

46. *Ibid.,* pp. 1b–2a.

47. Chang Tsu-lien, *Ting-an hsien-sheng nien-p'u wai-chi*, pp. 1a–b, in *Chüan-ching-lou ts'ung-k'o* (Shanghai, 1921), vol. IV.

48. *Ibid.*, p. 3a.

49. *Ibid.*, p. 2a.

50. See Chu Chieh-ch'in, *op. cit.*, chaps. 5 and 6, and pp. 104–5.

51. The "Five Mountains" are the five famous peaks located respectively in central, eastern, western, southern, and northern China. Kung uses the mountains in this poem as an analogy for the accumulation of his collections and writings on archaeology and epigraphy.

52. K 519.

53. K 553. Starting with Kung Tzu-chen and Wei Yüan, there was a tendency among the New Text scholars of late Ch'ing times to subscribe to Buddhism, which influenced the reformers of the 1890s: K'ang Yu-wei, T'an Ssu-t'ung, and Liang Ch'i-ch'ao. See Liang Ch'i-ch'ao, *op. cit.*, p. 73.

54. This poem and the above two are all from the *Miscellaneous Poems of the Year Chi-hai*.

55. Cf. Wang Kuo-wei, *Jen-chien tz'u-hua*, in T'ang Kuei-chang, ed., *Tz'u-hua ts'ung-pien* (Taipei, 1967), XII: 4268, and Ch'ien Mu, *Chung-kuo chin san-pai-nien hsüeh-shu shih*, p. 552.

56. "Divination shop" translates *pu-ssu*. I have added the word "hermit's" in this line because of the highly possible allusion to Yen Chün-p'ing of Han times who lived in seclusion in Ch'eng-tu and divined for a living. He only accepted several clients a day. After he had enough money to maintain himself for that day, he would close his shop, let down a screen, and study the *Lao tzu*. Yang Hsiung in his youth had studied under him.

57. Wang Kuo-wei, *Kang-t'ang ch'ang-tuan chü*, p. 7, in Ch'en Nai-ch'ien, ed., *Ch'ing ming-chia tz'u* (Hong Kong, 1963), vol. X.

58. K 89–90.

59. E.g. Ch'iu Yü-lin, *op. cit.*, chüan 5, p. 29; Chou Shao, "T'an Kung Ting-an," in *Jen-chien-shih*, XXXV (1935): 15; and Yao Shih-ju, "Kung Ting-an," pt. II, *Chung-yang jih-pao*, March 3, 1960. Both Ch'iu and Yao refer to Ling-hsiao simply as Kung's favorite; Chou, however, refers to her as a prostitute. Chu Chieh-ch'in, *op. cit.*, p. 81, says it is not known who Ling-hsiao was. But in *"Shang-ch'ing chen-jen pei shu-hou,"* K 298, Kung mentions a lady of Ku-su by the name of A-hsiao being in attendance on him when he wrote this piece. According to a footnote by the editor, A-hsiao was also called Ling-hsiao and was Kung's concubine.

60. Cf. Hsiao I-shan, *Ch'ing-tai t'ung-shih* (Taipei, 1963), IV: 1768, and *Kung Ting-an ch'üan-chi lei-pien* (Taipei, 1960), p. 373, editor's note to the first poem on the page.

61. K 518, two poems about Ling-hsiao; 518–19, three about Hsiao-yün; 528, two more about Ling-hsiao.

62. For an account of I-hui and Ku-t'ai-ch'ing, see Hummel, *op. cit.*, I: 386–87. The fact that they enjoyed a happy marriage can be illustrated by the poems they wrote in response to each other and by the names they

chose. T'ai-ch'ing was actually a sobriquet Ku took for herself to match I-hui's sobriquet, T'ai-su. The titles of their collected works also matched, especially that of her *tz'u* collection, *Fisherman's Songs of the Eastern Sea* (*Tung-hai yü-ko*), which parallels his *tz'u* collection, *Woodcutter Ditties of the Southern Valley* (*Nan-ku ch'iao-ch'ang*). They also happened to have been born in the same year.

63. Yeh-lai was another name for Hsüeh Ling-yün, a beautiful concubine of Ts'ao P'i, Emperor Wen of the Wei dynasty.

64. Meng Sen, *Hsin-shih ts'ung-k'an* (Shanghai, 1936), III: 40a.

65. "Dressed in white" translates *kao-i*, which derives from the *Book of Songs*; see Arthur Waley, *The Book of Songs* (New York: Grove Press, 1960), p. 43, No. 36. Chu Hsi interprets the term as the dress of a woman from a poor family. This is the interpretation followed by most commentators, including Meng Sen who thinks this refers to Kung's wife. However, the Mao commentaries to the *Book of Songs* interpret it as a white garment for men. In this case, it may refer to Kung himself. There is also the usage of *kao-i* as the white dress of mourning; this would make it a reference to Ku-t'ai-ch'ing after her husband's death. Since the poem itself does not indicate whether the letter was delivered from or to the vermilion mansion, all three interpretations are actually possible. In any case, this verse does show that Ku and Kung were on very friendly terms.

66. Tseng P'u, *Nieh-hai hua* (Peking, 1955), ch. 3, p. 17 to ch. 4, p. 22.

67. Meng Sen, *op. cit.*, pp. 41b–42a.

68. Ch'ien Mu, *Chung-kuo chin san-pai-nien hsüeh-shu shih*, p. 552. For Mu-chang-a, see Hummel, *op. cit.*, I: 582–83.

69. Wang Shou-nan, "Kung Tzu-chen hsien-sheng nien-p'u," *Ta-lu tsa-chih*, XVIII (1959), 9:28–29.

70. K 347, and Wang Shou-nan, *op. cit.*, 9:22.

71. Su Hsüeh-lin, "Ch'ing-tai nan-nü liang ta-tz'u-jen lien-shih te yen-chiu,"pt. II (Wu-han University), *Wen-che chi-k'an*, I: 4 (1931): 737–42. This article can also be found in *Wen-hsing ts'ung-k'an* (Taipei, 1967), No. 235, with a biographical account of Ku-t'ai-ch'ing appended.

72. K 598. It is ironic that in the minds of many Kung has come to typify a "literary dilettante."

73. K 564.

74. K 565.

75. Chu Chieh-ch'in, *op. cit.*, p. 106.

76. Tanaka, *op. cit.*, Preface, p. 29.

77. Su Hsüeh-lin, *op. cit.*, p. 743.

78. Tanaka, *op. cit.*, Preface, pp. 24–25.

79. This letter has not been included in the *Kung Tzu-chen ch'üan-chi*; see Yang Tien-shih, "Kung Tzu-chen chi-wai wen," in *Wen shih*, No. 2 (1963), p. 278.

Chapter Two

1. "Allegories," *yü-yen*, is a term from the *Chuang tzu*.
2. K 466.
3. K 470.
4. K 440.
5. "Overflowing words" is a translation of *chih-yen*, again a term from the *Chuang tzu*.
6. One such poem appears in K 482, one in K 490, five in K 496–97.
7. K 446.
8. "Ancient poet's" is a gloss for the term *ssu-shih* or "Four Beginnings," which refers to the first poems of the four sections of the *Book of Songs* and is here used to stand for the whole collection.
9. Many scholars have pointed out that dreams appear frequently in Kung's poems, but they have attempted little elucidation. For example, the dissertation on Kung by Annerose Wendhut, *Kung Tzu-chen: Leben und Werk* (University of Hamburg, 1953; n.p., 79 pp. of text proper with footnotes), mentions on pp. 73 and 75 the frequency of references to dreams but offers no explanation. Chu Chieh-ch'in, *op. cit.*, pp. 61–64, cites many of Kung's poems about dreams and sees in them an indication of the richness of the poet's imagination and sensitivity; he does not analyze the images in them. Tanaka, *op. cit.*, Preface, p. 8, ascribes the many dreams and reminiscences in Kung's poems to his unhappiness about existing situations and his spiritual turmoil.
10. See Kung's chronological biography, K 593.
11. K 466.
12. K 471, 472, 477, 483 respectively.
13. K 478–79, 481, 487–88.
14. The Chi-hai medley, written after Kung's retirement, contains a few quatrains about seeing his father again, enjoying the outdoors together, and presenting him with his latest poems; see K 524 and 537.
15. K 478.
16. Kung's occasional outbursts of pride and self-satisfaction can be illustrated by a poem commemorating his *tz'u* collection:

> Such restless intelligence and unusual talents
> Come, I suspect, from immortal sources;
> For the boon of a penetrating mind
> Could not possibly be an earthly gift.   [K 470]

There are a total of three quatrains in this cycle. They were found by Liu Ta-pai in a hand-copied edition of Kung's *tz'u*. See Liu's *Pai-wu shih-hua* (Taipei, 1957), pp. 75–78.
17. See the map of Peking at the end of Tanaka, *op. cit.*

18. *Tz'u yüan* (Shanghai, 1948), p. *mao* 112; Herbert A. Giles, *A Chinese Biographical Dictionary*, No. 321.

19. See Ch'ien Chung-shu, *T'an-i lu* (Hong Kong, 1965), p. 159.

20. "Words of Explanation" is a translation of *shih-yen*, a term which originates in the *Kuo yü* and is also the title of one of Han Yü's essays; see *Tz'u yüan*, p. *yu* 141.

21. "Aspiring" is the translation of *hsin-ch'i*. Though this term derives from the close friendship and mutual understanding between Hsiang Liu and Yen Chün, as recorded in the *Nan shih*, or *History of the Southern Dynasties*, it is used here only in a general sense with no specific reference to the original story. See *Tz'u yüan*, p. *mao* 2.

22. K 488.

23. Tanaka, *op. cit.*, Preface, pp. 25–27. See also Chu Chieh-ch'in, *op. cit.*, pp. 101–3, for some of Kung's writings on Buddhism.

24. For example, Hou Wai-lu, *op. cit.*, p. 626, who regrets that Kung studied the "Western books" too late in his life to write about them. By "Western" he must have meant European, since Kung did write a great deal on Buddhism. Such a misunderstanding of the term as applied to Kung has been pointed out by Chu Po-sung in "Kung Tzu-chen so-hao-te hsi-fang chih-shu shih shen-mo shu," *Kuang-ming jih-pao*, July 15, 1964.

25. *Wen-ni* is often rendered as *mou-ni*, probably due to a dialectic difference. In Cantonese, for instance, the character for "literature" (*wen*) is pronounced "mun" and therefore has the same initial sound as "mou"; it is probably interchangeable with "mou" for the purpose of transliteration.

26. "The historian" here refers to Pan Ku of the Han dynasty who was in charge of the Imperial Library, or *lan-t'ai* as given in Kung's text.

27. "Weaving Maid" is the Chinese name for the star Vega. "The south" translates *wei nan*, with *wei* interpreted as a particle, as is frequently the case in the *Book of Songs*.

28. To have "consumed the grain of the imperial granary" means to have drawn a salary from the government.

29. "Remote wild goose" translates *ming hung*, which derives from Yang Hsiung's observation, "The wild goose has flown far, far away. What can the archer gain?" "Wild goose" here implies a person who can detach himself from the world and therefore be free from interference and harm. The term has since been commonly used; see Tanaka, *op. cit.*, p. 163, and *Tz'u yüan*, pp. *tzu* 181 and *hai* 42. Kung, however, is questioning such an attitude of detachment.

30. This line alludes to the incident in the *Analects* (XVIII:6) where Confucius came across two recluses on the road and asked them the way. When it turned out that they did not understand why he did not withdraw from the world, the Master observed sadly: "A man cannot live with birds and beasts. Whom can I associate with but my fellow men? If the empire were in good order, I would not bother myself with government."

31. See Tanaka, *op. cit.*, p. 86, and Feng Yu-lan, *A Short History of Chinese Philosophy*, ed. Derk Bodde (New York: The Free Press, 1966), pp. 278–80.

32. For a handy reference, see *Tz'u yüan*, p. *ch'ou* 63.

33. See *Chin-tai shih-hsüan*, p. 29.

34. Tanaka, *op. cit.*, p. 86.

35. *Ibid.*, pp. 86–87.

36. *Tz'u yüan*, p. *tzu* 16.

37. *Ibid.*, p. *ch'en* 56.

38. K 440.

39. K 459–60.

40. K 469.

41. K 492–93.

42. This may allude to a piece of rhyme-prose, the *Teng-t'u-tzu hao-se fu*, in which Sung Yü tells of a beautiful girl living in the neighboring house to the east. Although for three years she had been peeping at him over the wall that separated their houses, she was unable to impress him.

43. In the life stories of outstanding monks, it is often said that the mother dreamed of the moon entering her breast before she became pregnant; see Tanaka, *op. cit.*, p. 17. There are also non-Buddhist references to the same phenomenon; see the *Yüan-chien lei-han, chüan* 3, "moon entries," section II: the mother of Empress Wang of the Han dynasty, the wife of Sun Chien of the Three Kingdoms, and the mother of Emperor Yüan of the Liang dynasty each dreamed that the moon had dropped into her breast before giving birth to an extraordinary child.

44. "Heart's History" (*Hsin shih*), the title of a collection of poems by Cheng Ssu-hsiao of Sung-Yüan times, is full of patriotic feeling for the fallen Sung dynasty; see *Tz'u yüan*, p. *mao* 1. Kung may have had this specific reference in mind, or he may simply have used the term in the general sense of personal history.

45. See n. 42 above.

46. See n. 29 above.

47. Kung began his service in 1820, at the age of twenty-nine, as a secretary in the Grand Secretariat. The following year he became a redactor in the Grand Secretariat's Bureau of Dynastic History and participated in the revision of the *General Gazetteer of the Ch'ing Empire (Ta-ch'ing i-t'ung chih)*.

48. "Abstruse philosophies," a gloss for "trend of the Chin masters," refers to the Taoist philosophical discussions in vogue during Wei-Chin times. Sometimes known as "lofty talks," or *ch'ing-t'an*, they tend to shun practical issues.

Chapter Three

1. For the rules governing *lü-shih*, or regulated verse, see James J. Y. Liu, *The Art of Chinese Poetry* (Chicago: University of Chicago Press, 1966), pp. 26–28.

2. Some editions note that this series was written as a result of failing the examination for the Privy Council. It cannot be determined whether this note was inserted by Kung himself or by a later compiler, though some sources treat it as the poet's; e.g., Wang Shou-nan, *op. cit.*, 8:25. Incidentally, this series marks the breaking of Kung's first vow, taken in the previous year, to abstain from writing poetry.

3. See *Tz'u yüan*, p. *ssu* 62.

4. Other examples include three quatrains to the Music Bureau tune *Tzu-yün hui*, K 449.

5. "Salt Ministry" translates *lao-p'en*, literally a utensil for heating salt.

6. See, e.g., *Chin-tai shih-hsüan*, pp. 22–23. Chang Yin-lin, taking the same radical approach to Kung, has actually interpreted *hsia-k'o* (patron at a brothel) as the emperor; see *Chang Yin-lin wen-chi* (Taipei, 1956), p. 169. This article deals mainly with the meaning of Kung's "Song of a Scholar of the Han Dynasty" (*Han-ch'ao ju-sheng hsing*) and originally appeared in *Yen-ching hsüeh-pao*, XIII (1933): 203–8.

7. See Tai Hung-sen's article on the interpretation of two of Kung's poems, "Tsen-yang chieh-shih Kung Tzu-chen te liang-shou shih," in *Kuang-ming jih-pao*, July 12, 1964.

8. For a brief biographical account of Tseng Yü, see *Chung-kuo wen-hsüeh-chia ta tz'u-tien*, No. 6361.

9. K 610–11.

10. See Ch'ien Mu, *Kuo-shih ta-kang*, II: 603.

11. K 452–53.

12. The Feng-i Gate was to the southwest of the Yu-an Gate outside Peking; see *Chin-tai shih-hsüan*, p. 27, and the map at the end of Tanaka, *op. cit.*

13. K'un-yang is located in present-day Honan Province. In the 23 A.D. battle fought there between Liu Hsiu and Wang Mang, the latter was utterly defeated.

14. "Goddesses" is a translation of *t'ien-nü*, female Buddhist deities. Eighty-four thousand is a number which frequently occurs in Buddhist scriptures in connection with great quantities.

15. The Taoists believe that between the human world and the palace of the Jade Emperor there are thirty-six different heavenly strata.

16. The *Tripitaka*, the three divisions of the Buddhist Canon, consists of the sermons of the Buddha, monastic rules, and discussions on dogma.

17. The *Vimalakirti Sutra*, short for *Vimalakirti-nirdesa Sutra*, is an apocryphal account of the conversations between Shakyamuni and some residents of Vaisali, the native place of Vimalakirti.

18. Tanaka, *op. cit.*, p. 108.

19. *Tz'u yüan*, p. *hai* 82.

20. Western Mountain refers to the mountain ranges northwest of Peking. Many Buddhist temples are located there; see Tanaka, *op. cit.*, p. 38.

21. "A raft crossing the Milky Way" derives from the story of a fisherman who reached the Milky Way by boarding a raft which floated by in the eighth month of each year; see, for instance, the Chinese commentaries to Tu Fu's "Autumn Meditation" (Ch'iu-hsing pa-shou), No. 2, or the footnote to this poem regarding "the raft which came by this eighth month" in A. C. Graham, Poems of the Late T'ang (Baltimore: Penguin Books, 1965), pp. 55–56.

22. "Emperer Star" is a translation of Ti-tso which refers to the second star in the Polar Constellation. This star was supposed to symbolize the emperor on earth; see Chin-tai shih-hsüan, p. 19.

23. "The propitious air of heroines" is a translation of ch'i-nü ch'i. This expression derives from a story in the Han shu, or Dynastic History of the [Former] Han Dynasty, according to which Emperor Wu met one of his favorite ladies by following the omen of propitious air in the sky. In this poem, Kung was probably anticipating the appearance of extraordinary women to rescue the country. See Tanaka, op. cit., p. 50.

24. "Constellation of Scholars" is a translation of shao-wei hsing, a constellation which was supposed to symbolize scholars without official rank; see ibid., p. 51. It is not clear whether Kung had any specific scholar in mind. "Fallen" suggests death. He might be referring to the lack of vitality of scholars in the south, and therefore he hoped that some outstanding women would rise and take over the leadership.

25. "Queries to Heaven" refers to Ch'ü Yüan's T'ien wen, which raises many questions about ancient history, mythology, and the universe. Here, Kung is saying that he does not express his grievances by questioning heaven.

26. K 465, 456, 447–48.

27. K 440, 445, 456.

28. Cleanth Brooks, The Well Wrought Urn (New York: Harcourt, Brace & World, 1947), p. 127.

29. Liang Ch'i-ch'ao, Chung-kuo yün-wen li-t'ou so piao-hsien te ch'ing-kan (Taipei, 1958), p. 50.

30. "Flowers swaying in the wind" is a translation of feng-hua, which refers to prostitutes.

31. K 460–62. For speculations on the central figure in this poem, see Chang Yin-lin, op. cit., pp. 165–70 and 462.

32. See Aoki Masaru's book on the history of literary criticism in the Ch'ing dynasty, Shindai bungaku hyōron shi, translated by Ch'en Shu-nü as Ch'ing-tai wen-hsüeh p'ing-lun shih (Taipei, 1969), p. 24.

33. Chang Wen-t'ao, Chang ch'uan-shan shih-chi (Shanghai, 1936), p. 145, No. 7 of the eight quatrains entitled "On Literature" (Lun wen).

Chapter Four

1. K 353. A Chinese mile (li) is about one-third of an English mile.

2. Yang Tsai, Shih-fa chia-shu, chüan 2, in Shih-hsüeh chih-nan (Taipei, 1970), p. 32.

3. Wang Shih-chen (of Ming), *I-yüan chih-yen, chüan* 1, p. 8b, in Ting Fu-pao, ed., *Hsü li-tai shih-hua* (Taipei, 1971), vol. III. Wang's observation reminds us of William Blake's poetic reflection of "a world in a grain of sand" ("Auguries of Innocence," line 1).

4. Liu Hsi-tsai, *I kai, chüan* 2 (Taipei, 1969), pp. 14a–b.

5. Shen Te-ch'ien, *Shuo-shih tsui-yü*, pt. I, in *Ch'ing shih-hua* (Shanghai, 1963), II: 542.

6. I refer to Wang Shih-chen of the Ch'ing dynasty by his sobriquet in order to distinguish him from the Wang Shih-chen of Ming times.

7. Wang Yü-yang, *Shih-yu shih-ch'uan hsü-lu*, in *Ch'ing shih-hua*, I: 150.

8. For the various opinions of Tu Fu's *chüeh-chü*, see my article, "The Quatrains of Tu Fu," *Monumenta Serica*, XXIX (1970–71): 142–62.

9. Hu Ying-lin, *Shih sou*, pt., I, *chüan* 6, p. 6b, in *Shao-shih shan-fang pi-ts'ung* (Kuang-ya Bookstore, 1896 ed.).

10. Wang Fu-chih, *Chiang-chai shih-hua*, pt. II, in *Ch'ing shih-hua*, I: 20. Conclusive evidence of the existence of the *chüeh-chü* before the maturation of the *lü-shih* in T'ang times can be seen in the fact that many five-character *chüeh-chü* were collected into the *Yü-t'ai hsin-yung* by Hsü Ling (507–583). They also appear in various chapters of the *History of the Southern Dynasties (Nan shih)*. For further information on the origin and development of the *chüeh-chü*, see Hung Wei-fa, *Chüeh-chü lun* (Shanghai, 1934).

11. Wang Fu-chih, *op. cit.*, I: 18.

12. Ssu-k'ung T'u, *Ssu-k'ung Piao-sheng wen-chi, chüan* 2 (*Ssu-pu ts'ung-k'an* ed.), p. 3a.

13. Chang Yen, *Tz'u yüan*, pt. II (Hong Kong, 1968), p. 7a.

14. Yang Tsai, *loc. cit.*

15. Shih Pu-hua, *Hsien-yung shuo-shih*, in *Ch'ing shih-hua*, II: 996–97.

16. Hu Ying-lin, *op. cit.*, p. 7a.

17. *Ibid.*, p. 12a.

18. Shen Te-ch'ien, *T'ang-shih pieh-ts'ai, chüan* 19 (Shanghai, 1958), p. 116.

19. Hu Ying-lin, *op. cit.*, p. 14b.

20. For example, Chang Meng-chi, *Chin-t'i-shih fa-fan* (Taipei, 1970), p. 26; and Ma Fu-chün, "Ku-shih ti han-hsü piao-hsien-fa," *Ch'u-pan yüeh-k'an*, II: 11 (Apr. 1967): 84.

21. Yü Ta-fu, "T'an shih," in *Hsien shu* (Shanghai, 1936), pp. 167–68.

22. "Eastern Hills" (*Tung shan*) and "Northern Hills" (*Pei shan*), the titles of two poems in the *Book of Songs*, lament the plight of soldiers and officials separated from their families. Kung might have intended these two terms to be subtle allusions to his personal experience of leaving the capital without bringing his family with him.

23. Tu Fu, for example, has compared Ch'ang-an to a chessboard in his "Autumn Meditation," No. 4; see Graham, *op. cit.*, p. 53.

24. *Tz'u yüan*, p. *tzu* 17.

25. To this day, in fact, a commemorative landmark called the Rain Flower Terrace (*Yü-hua t'ai*) exists in the vicinity of Nanking, the ancient Chiang-ning district.

26. Wang Yü-yang, *Shih-yu shih-ch'uan hsü-lu*, in *Ch'ing shih-hua*, I: 155. According to *Tz'u hai* (Shanghai, 1948), p. 1097, *huo-chü* ("sentence with life") refers to meaningless sentences which Zen masters use to initiate their disciples; sentences with meaning are called *ssu-chü* ("dead sentences"). Professor Hsiao Kung-ch'üan has suggested to me that *huo-chü* might be taken as "amphibolous and metonymical verses." For discussions of the application of this term in the context of poetry, see Kuo Shao-yü, *Ts'ang-lang shih-hua chiao-shih* (Peking, 1962), pp. 116–17; Ch'ien Chung-shu, *op. cit.*, pp. 117–18, 367–68, 374.

27. "No longer worn" is a gloss for *pu ju shih*, which may mean either "not comparable to the vogue" or "do not go to the market-place." A passage in ch. 129 (*Huo-chih lieh-chuan*) of Ssu-ma Ch'ien's (145–86? B.C.) *Shih chi* (*Records of the Grand Historian*) reads: "In the poor people's quest for affluence, farmers are not comparable to artisans, artisans are not comparable to merchants, and doing needlework is not comparable to prostitution [literally: "leaning on the city gate"—*i shih-men*]." In this poem, Kung might be borrowing part of the terminology from the last line: *pu-ju i shih-men*, without following its meaning.

28. This is another allusion to a passage in ch. 129 of the *Shih chi* where the women of Chao are described as wearing "sharp-pointed slippers." A commentary to this passage interprets these as dancing shoes. Professor Lao Kan informs me that such dancing shoes had nothing to do with foot binding, which was not practiced until Southern Sung times. It is hard to tell whether Kung Tzu-chen has mistaken these slippers as evidence of foot binding or has simply used the term "sharp-pointed slippers" figuratively.

29. "Virtue's reputation" (*hui yin*) derives from No. 240 of the *Book of Songs:* "And T'ai-ssu carried on her fair name [*hui yin*], / Bearing a multitude of sons" (as translated in Waley, *op. cit.*, p. 260).

30. This interpretation follows that of Ch'ien Mu; see *Chung-kuo chin san-pai-nien hsüeh-shu shih*, p. 545.

31. This line derives from the "Summons of the Soul" (*Chao hun*) in the *Songs of the South* (*Ch'u tz'u*): "Tigers and leopards guard the nine gates, ever ready to rend up mortal men." (The translation is adopted from David Hawkes, *The Songs of the South*, Beacon Paperback ed., p. 105.) The concluding note of gratitude and hope in Kung's poem recalls one of his letters to a friend in which he also speaks of himself in terms of fallen flowers and alludes to Wu Wei-yeh's "The Song of Yüan-yüan" (*Yüan-yüan ch'ü*): "The violent wind has been wrongly blamed for scattering the blossoms; / Behold the glory of spring fills heaven and earth." [K 349] For in the end, Ch'en Yüan-yüan was rescued from the bandits by Wu San-kuei (1612–78).

32. This refers to writings which are worthy of being collected and preserved at monasteries.

33. It is commonly believed that Taoist immortals ride on cranes. The implication here is that someone in a high position condescends to communicate with the poet.

34. "Mate of the recluse" alludes to the story of the Sung poet Lin Pu (965?–1026) who spent his life in retirement on a hill near the West Lake; he considered the plum blossom his wife and the crane his son. See *Tz'u yüan*, p. *ch'en* 81.

35. "Gold" here can be taken either literally as money or figuratively as the value of friendship. Judging from what Kung says in poem No. 94 about his material wants at this time, one finds the literal interpretation more appropriate, for it underscores his desperation; however, the figurative sense of "gold" probably fits better into the context of the piece.

Chapter Five

1. For further information on these three quatrians, see ch. 2, n. 16.

2. See Kung's chronological biography in K 595, 606, 626.

3. In a note to No. 75 of his Chi-hai quatrains, Kung expressed regret for having preserved his *tz'u* works at all. The poem itself speaks very apologetically of the quality of his *tz'u:*

> Not having archaic refinement or subtle inspiration,
> A style hardly merits ascent to the writers' hall:
> I regret leaving them for the sing-song girls,
> And conceal myself behind a silk fan as I pass
>   the wine pavilion. [K 516]

"The wine pavilion" alludes to a widely circulated anecdote involving three famous T'ang poets: Wang Ch'ang-ling, Kao Shih, and Wang Chih-huan. One day the three poets gathered at a wine pavilion to drink. Shortly afterwards, some entertainers and sing-song girls arrived. As it was the custom for the show girls to put to music the recent compositions of well-known poets, the three friends secretly agreed to keep track of how many of their own poems would be selected by these singers. Before long, the girls sang one of Kao Shih's poems and then two of Wang Ch'ang-ling's; but they sang none of Wang Chih-huan's. Thereupon, Wang Chih-huan pointed to the most attractive girl in the group and said to his friends: "If what she sings does not turn out to be one of my poems, I shall never dare to compete with you two again." Lo and behold, the girl did sing Wang's masterpiece: "The Yellow River climbs far into the white clouds. . . . " See *Tz'u yüan*, p. *mao* 122.

4. See Glen Baxter, "Metrical Origin of the *Tz'u*," *Harvard Journal of Asiatic Studies*, XVI (1953): 108–45; and Irving Lo, *Hsin Ch'i-chi* (New York: Twayne Publishers, 1971), ch. 2: "The Evolution of the Lyric Meter."

5. This depreciative attitude toward the *tz'u* can be seen even in defenses made on its behalf, many of which begin by conceding that the *tz'u* is a minor genre: see Wu Hung-i, *Ch'ang-chou p'ai tz'u-hsüeh yen-chiu* (Taipei, 1970), pp. 35–36. The ambivalent attitude of Kung Tzu-chen's maternal grandfather, the famous philologist Tuan Yu-ts'ai, is a case in point. In his youth, Tuan was also fond of composing *tz'u*, but gave up the practice after being admonished by his father that absorption in *tz'u* is detrimental to the pursuit of the classics. Fifty years later, when Tuan read the *tz'u* collections of his grandson, he was struck with admiration for the excellence of the work. Yet, in spite of his admiration, Tuan in turn admonished the young poet not to indulge in a literary endeavor which would only distract him from the cultivation of the self. (See K 597.) It was such a basic distrust of the didactic value of the *tz'u* which prompted Chang Hui-yen and the Ch'ang-chou School to insist that the inclusion of hidden messages in *tz'u* would elevate the status of the genre.

6. For example, the Ming critic Yü Yen (c. 1615) explained the meaning of *shih-yü* in terms of historical evolution: *tz'u* came after the decline of *shih* when the musical accompaniment for the latter had already been lost; the implication is that *yü* means "after," so that *shih-yü* means that *tz'u* came "after" *shih* chronologically. On the other hand, K'uang Chou-i (1859–1926) of late Ch'ing times thought that both *shih* and *tz'u* are synchronically related to music, and that *yü* refers to the prosodic lengthening of the *shih* form; thus, *yü* has a musical rather than chronological significance. See I Chün-tso, *Chung-kuo wen-hsüeh shih* (Taipei, 1964), p. 234, and Hsia Ch'eng-t'ao and Wu Hsiung-ho, *Tu-tz'u ch'ang-shih* (Hong Kong, n.d.), pp. 10–12.

7. These four collections contain a total of 103 *tz'u*.

8. See K 606. With regard to the meaning of the term "red *dhyāna*," the poet has only one obscure reference to it in No. 2 of a cycle of three quatrains written at the end of this collection: "As for the meaning of the term 'red *dhyāna*,' / Red is the next life and *dhyāna* this life." [K 470]

9. The two stanzas here are actually a reduplication of the tune "Autumn in the Cassia Hall" (*Kuei tien ch'iu*), which has only four lines.

As for the tune titles themselves, Kung often cites variant titles for the same tune; for example, "Waves Washing over Sand" is the same tune as "The Flower-Seller's Song," and "Moon on the Hsiang River" is the same tune as "The Hundred-Word Ditty." For the sake of clarity and the convenience of reference, the translations of tune titles in this chapter are strictly the choice of the author in each case.

10. The West Pond alludes to the mythological abode of the fairy queen Hsi Wang-mu; Green Phoenix is her messenger bird.

11. Incidentally, the descriptive details of these dream poems have led many literal-minded critics to indulge in the extremes of biographical reading. It has been suggested that Kung is reliving in these dream pieces

an actual love affair; in fact, efforts have been made to identify the locality and the central figure of the recurrent dreams. See, for example, the discussions in Su Hsüeh-lin's article mentioned in ch. 1, n. 71. The purpose of the present chapter is to show that such factual reading does not do justice to a versatile poet.

12. "Shed her pendants" may allude to *chieh-p'ei;* see *Tz'u yüan*, p. *yu* 7. "Stockinged feet" alludes to the rhyme-prose "The Goddess of the Lo" *(Lo-shen fu)* by Ts'ao Chih (192–232), in which the goddess walks daintily on the waves: "Traversing the waves in tiny steps,/ Her gauze slippers *(lo wa)* seem to stir a dust." (Quoted from Burton Watson, *Chinese Rhyme-Prose*, New York: Columbia University Press, 1971, p. 59.)

13. "Smoke and ashes" refers to Su Shih's famour *tz'u* on the Battle of Red Cliff ("The great river flows east . . . "), in which boats and masts went up in flame as the victors laughed and chatted among themselves. To mention Su Shih and Li Po together may give the impression that I am questioning Professor Kōjirō Yoshikawa's thesis that the Sung poets, Su Shih in particular, have distinguished themselves in the annals of Chinese poetry by their many-sided interests, and that the basic antithesis between T'ang and Sung poetry lies in the former's immersion in sorrow and the latter's transcendental outlook which views "human life as a thing of long duration, a process of quiet resistance." (See Kōjirō Yoshikawa, *An Introduction to Sung Poetry*, trans. Burton Watson; Cambridge: Harvard University Press, 1967; p. 26.) Actually, this is not the case at all. I am merely trying to hear the less "quiet" voice of Su Shih. And it may not be inappropriate to point out that even Professor Yoshikawa himself qualifies his theme of transcendence with expressions such as "at least" (pp. 25, 27, 32, 35), "not . . . completely" (p. 31), and "not wholly successful" (p. 109).

14. "Little Su" *(Su-hsiao)* was a famous courtesan at Ch'ien-t'ang during the Six Dynasties. Her grave is in Chia-hsing district, Chekiang. Later, however, people made another grave for her at Hangchow along the northern shore of West Lake. See Cheng Ch'ien, *Hsü tz'u-hsüan* (Taipei, 1955), p. 146.

15. "Prince Ch'ien" refers to Ch'ien Liu, ruler of the Kingdom of Wu-yüeh during the Five Dynasties. He was a native of Hangchow. See *Tz'u yüan*, p. *hsü* 22.

16. K 597–98; Wang Shou-nan, *op. cit.,* 7: 14–15.

17. One of the two friends, Sun Lin-chih, was an established *tz'u* poet and supporter of the Che-hsi School; see Aoki Masaru, *op. cit.,* pp. 194, 202; T'an Hsien, *Fu-t'ang tz'u-hua,* in T'ang Kuei-chang, ed., *op cit.,* XI: 4023; and Chiang Jun-hsün, *Tz'u-hsüeh p'ing-lun-shih kao* (Hong Kong, 1966), pp. 246–49.

18. T'an Hsien, *op. cit.,* p. 4022.

19. See Cheng Ch'ien, *Ts'ung shih tao ch'ü* (Taipei, 1961), pp. 104–5.

20. See, for example, the opinion of Li Tz'u-ming in *Yüeh-man-t'ang*

tu-shu chi (Peking, 1963), II: 877. According to Wang Li's *Han-yü shih-lü hsüeh*, Wan Shu's *Tz'u lü*, and Ch'a Wang-wang's *Tz'u-hsüeh ch'üan-shu*, the following *tz'u* translated in this chapter contain prosodic violations: "Dreaming of a Beauty"; "The Long Tune on the Magnolia Blossom"; and the "Gold Thread Song."

21. In T'ang Kuei-chang, ed., *op. cit.*, XI: 3800–2.

22. For a translation of the entire *tz'u*, see Irving Lo, *op. cit.*, p. 123.

23. *Ibid.*, pp. 100–4, 128–32.

24. See Cheng Ch'ien, *Ts'ung shih tao ch'ü*, p. 162 ff.

25. For example, in Ho Kuang-chung, *Lun Ch'ing tz'u* (Singapore, 1958), pp. 18, 22, Kung's *tz'u* is categorized as a variation of the Che-hsi style; in Aoki, *op. cit.*, pp. 181–82, Kung is grouped with the Ch'ang-chou School. On the other hand, I Chün-tso, *op. cit.*, p. 428, considers Kung an independent *tz'u* poet.

26. Samples of the *tz'u* of Nara Singde and Chiang Ch'un-lin have been translated by William Schultz and Cyril Birch, respectively, in Cyril Birch, ed., *Anthology of Chinese Literature*, Vol. II (New York: Grove Press, 1972), pp. 143–49, 291–92. For the translation of one of Ch'en Wei-sung's *tz'u* and four of Chu I-tsun's, see *ibid.*, pp. 138–42.

27. Aoki, *op. cit.*, pp. 194–95.

28. Wu Hung-i, *op. cit.*, pp. 24–25; Ho Kuang-chung, *op. cit.*, pp. 1–2, 10–13, 31–42.

29. Wu Hung-i, *op. cit.*, pp. 17–23; Ho Kuang-chung, *op. cit.*, pp. 43–44; Aoki, *op. cit.*, pp. 186–91.

30. Chiang Jun-hsün, *op. cit.*, pp. 226–32; Aoki, *op. cit.*, pp. 195–200. The phrase *i-nei yen-wai* ("meaning within, language without") was used in the *Shuo wen* to define the term *tz'u* as "words." Chang Hui-yen apparently borrowed the expression out of context to define the term *tz'u* as "lyrics." Though the character is the same, the connotation is different in each case; see Wu Hung-i, *op. cit.*, pp. 40–41, 110.

31. Wu Hung-i, *op. cit.*, pp. 25–26, 36–37.

32. *Ibid.*, pp. 18, 21; Chiang Jun-hsün, *op. cit.*, p. 206.

33. Chang Hui-yen, *Tz'u hsüan*, in the *Cheng-hsü tz'u-hsüan* (Shanghai, 1935), p. 19. The Chinese text and a complete translation of this *tz'u* can be found in Alan Ayling and Duncan Mackintosh, *A Collection of Chinese Lyrics* (New York: Chelsea House Publishers, 1965), pp. 114–15.

34. Chou Chi, *Chieh-ts'un-chai lun-tz'u tsa-chu*, in T'ang Kuei-chang, ed., *op. cit.*, V: 1624.

35. Chou Chi, *Sung ssu-chia tz'u-hsüan*, Preface, *ibid.*, p. 1630.

36. "Delicate streamers" translates *ch'ing-fan*, a term which may allude to the variegated "spring streamers" (*ch'un-fan*) on display in the beginning of spring (see *Tz'u yüan*, p. *ch'en* 12). Su Shih has a *tz'u* to the tune of *Chien-tzu mu-lan-hua* which, like Chang Hui-yen's, also mentions "spring streamers" together with willow catkins.

37. The comparison of green duckweeds to "spots of teardrops congealed" is obviously inspired by Su Shih. In an authorial note to a *tz'u* on the same subject of willow catkins (to the tune of *Shui lung yin*), Su observes that the duckweeds result from the metamorphosis of willow catkins. This explains the otherwise not very clear relationship between catkins, duckweeds, and teardrops in Chang's piece. Su Shih's poem can be found in the *Tz'u hsüan* compiled by Chang, and in Ayling and Mackintosh, *op. cit.*, pp. 122–23.

38. See n. 20 above; for the prosodic violations in Chang Hui-yen's piece, see Cheng Ch'ien, *Hsü tz'u-hsüan*, p. 141.

39. T'ang Kuei-chang, ed., *op. cit.*, XI: 4023.

40. "Little song-form" (*hsiao yüeh-fu*) refers to the *tz'u*.

41. See Ho Kuang-chung, *op. cit.*, p. 15. For samples of their *tz"u*, see appendix to Chang Hui-yen's *Tz'u hsüan*.

42. The Seven-Miles Rapids was near the place where Yen Kuang of the Later Han lived. Yen was a good friend of Emperor Kuang-wu, but he refused to take any political office. (See Yen's biography in the *Hou Han shu*.) Li O wrote this *tz'u* in admiration of the reclusive life.

43. The "dream about the crane" alludes to Su Shih's second *fu* on the Red Cliff; he saw a crane while he was boating at night and afterwards had a dream about the bird.

44. "The fisherman of the western cliff" alludes to a poem by the T'ang poet Liu Tsung-yüan which begins with the line "A fisherman rests by the western cliff at night." This fisherman symbolizes carefree living. The endings of the two pieces are very similar.

45. Hsi-she was a society for the composition of *tz'u* formed by Sung loyalists at the beginning of the Yüan dynasty. Many of its members were from Li O's native province, Chekiang.

46. Chiang Jun-hsün, *op. cit.*, p. 205.

47. K 597.

Chapter Six

1. The eighteenth-century poet Yüan Mei (1716–98), for instance, gave up a budding career without any visible signs of agony. At the age of thirty-three, Yüan bowed out of officialdom, purchased an estate near Nanking, and retreated into his garden of pleasure. Later, Yüan expounded in his *Sui-yüan shih-hua (Poetry Talks from the Sui Garden)* a quasi-romantic view of poetry which exalts spontaneous expression and individual temperament, a poetic view consonant with his hedonistic outlook on life. For Yüan's life and literary outlook, see Arthur Waley's biographical study, *Yüan Mei: Eighteenth-Century Chinese Poet* (New York: Grove Press Inc., 1956), especially pp. 46–47, 57, 68, 78–80, 82, 127, 144, 166–67, 203–4. For a discussion of Yüan's conception of poetry within the Chinese critical framework, see James Liu, *The Art of Chinese Poetry*, pp. 70–76.

2. "A priceless sword" translates *ch'ien-chin chien*, a term used here to stand for reciprocal friendship even at the price of parting with one's most treasured possession. The term may allude to a story recorded in the *Shih chi* involving two friends and a rare sword. The owner of the sword (whose name was Chi Cha) had secretly pledged the sword to a friend, but had to keep it until he completed a diplomatic round. Meanwhile, the friend had died. Upon his return from the diplomatic mission, Chi Cha went to the friend's burial site and redeemed his pledge by hanging the sword on a tree by the grave. See *Tz'u yüan*, p. *mao* 72.

3. The question is probably unanswerable, since any attempt at placing a poet historically inevitably results either in a facile judgment or an enormous task of reexamining an entire poetic history.

4. The condemnatory words are those of Chang Ping-lin, quoted in Ch'ien Chi-po. *Hsien-tai Chung-kuo wen-hsüeh shih* (Hong Kong, 1965 reprint) pp. 72–73. Interestingly, Liang Ch'i-ch'ao, who acknowledges Kung's contribution to Ch'ing thought (see Chapter One), also finds mid-Ch'ing poets, Kung included, "crude and shallow." (See Liang Ch'i-ch'ao, *Ch'ing-tai hsüeh-shu kai-lun*, p. 75.) Nevertheless, as we shall see, Liang and his fellow reformers often borrowed Kung's lines.

5. Ch'ing *shih* is on the whole highly imitative in nature; the poets went through "revival" phases in which they would either adopt the simple lyricism of T'ang or imitate the narrative quality of Sung. (See Liu Ta-chieh, *Chung-kuo wen-hsüeh fa-chan shih*, Hong Kong, 1964, III: 281–92.) Kung Tzu-chen wrote during a transitional, innovative period, and is considered an "independent" poet with a creative personal style. See Hsi Che, *Chung-kuo shih-tz'u yen-chin shih* (Hong Kong, 1954), p. 100; Chang Tsung-hsiang, *Ch'ing-tai wen-hsüeh* (Hong Kong, 1964), p. 38; and Ch'ien O-sun, "Che-p'ai shih-lun," *Hsüeh-shu shih-chieh*, I (1935), 5:64–65.

6. Since Kung's *tz'u* and its relationship with earlier *tz'u* poetry have already been discussed in the previous chapter, the observations in this chapter pertain to his *shih* poetry only.

7. Kurata Sadayoshi, *Chugoku kindai shi no kenkyu* (Tokyo, 1969), p. 524; Chu Chieh-ch'in, *op. cit.*, pp. 83, 98.

8. Chu Chieh-ch'in, *op. cit.*, pp. 98–99.

9. Ching K'o was a famous would-be assassin of the third century B.C.; Chu-ko Liang was a loyal statesman of the Three Kingdoms period. See Giles, *op. cit.*, Nos. 399 and 459.

10. For a general discussion of T'ao Ch'ien's themes and imagery, see Huang Chung-lun, *T'ao Yüan-ming tso-p'in yen-chiu* (Taipei, 1969), pp. 8–22. For discussions of the bird symbol, see J. R. Hightower, *The Poetry of T'ao Ch'ien* (Oxford: Clarendon Press, 1970), pp. 15, 40, 84, 89, 95–96, 129, 130, 133–34, 146, 203–4; for the pine tree/cypress symbol, see pp. 113–15, 136, 178, 202; for the farmer's life, see pp. 50–56, 108, 229–30.

11. Chu Chieh-ch'in, *op. cit.*, p. 100.

12. For examples of Lu Yu's use of parallelism, see Chao I, *Ou-pei shih-hua* (Shanghai, 1917), *chüan* 6, pp. 3b–13a; and Liu Wei-ch'ung, *Lu Yu p'ing-chuan* (Taipei, 1966), pp. 406–16.

13. Ch'ien Chung-shu, *op. cit.*, pp. 152–53; Yoshikawa, *op. cit.*, pp. 146–47, 154–58; and Burton Watson, tr., *The Old Man Who Does as He Pleases: Selections from the Poetry and Prose of Lu Yu* (New York: Columbia University Press, 1973).

14. See Kurata, *loc. cit.*; Chu Chieh-ch'in, *op. cit.*, pp. 99–100; Ling Shan-ch'ing, ed., *P'ing-chu ch'ing-shih tu-pen* (Shanghai, 1932), II: 114; and Kanda Kiichirō, "Kyo Tei-an no 'Ch'iu-yeh t'ing Yü Ch'iu-p'u t'an p'i-p'a' no shi ni tsuite," *Ishida hakushi shōju kinen tōyōshi ronsō* (1964), pp. 195–203.

15. K 466.

16. Chu Chieh-ch'in, *op. cit.*, p. 99; Ling Shan-ch'ing, *loc. cit.*; Kuo-hsüeh fu-lun she edition, *Kung Ting-an ch'üan-chi, wen-chi pu*, I: 9a.

17. Wang Yü-yang, *Jan-teng chi-wen*, in *Ch'ing shih-hua*, I: 119.

18. See Chu Ho-ling, ed., *Li I-shan shih-chi* (Taipei, 1967), pp. 200, 202, 232, 238, 378, and 356. For interpretation of the *luan* and *feng* allusions in Li Shang-yin's poetry, see Su Hsüeh-lin, *Yü-hsi shih-mi* (Taipei, 1958), pp. 62–68.

19. Chu Ho-ling, *op. cit.*, pp. 138, 350, 367; K 440, 441, 533. For the story of Tung-fang So, see James J. Y. Liu, *The Poetry of Li Shang-yin, Ninth-Century Baroque Chinese Poet* (Chicago: The University of Chicago Press, 1969), p. 97.

20. For discussion of Li's use of allusion and mythology, see *ibid.*, pp. 99–105, 109–113, 248.

21. *Ibid.*, p. 66.

22. *Ibid.*, pp. 67, 236–46.

23. *Ibid.*, p. 252.

24. A. C. Graham, *op. cit.*, p. 155.

25. Legend has it that Ch'ang O stole the magic herb from her husband in order to attain longevity, but ended up facing a life of eternal loneliness.

26. See Su Hsüeh-lin, *Yü-hsi shih-mi*, p. 18.

27. Arthur Waley, *The Poetry and Career of Li Po* (London: George Allen & Unwin, 1950), pp. 38–40.

28. *Ibid.*, p. 46.

29. Li Po's "Banished Immortal" image is an exaggerated posture. His political ambition is shown by his repeated attempts to enter public service. Although constantly speaking with the pride of a commoner, he was never slow to jump into the arena of political struggle whenever an opportunity came along. In fact, at the age of sixty he still frantically sought a metropolitan post. See *ibid.*, pp. 10, 84–86, 96.

30. As suggested, for example, by *Chung-kuo wen-hsüeh shih* (Peking, 1959), p. 605.

31. K 255.

32. Ch'ü Yüan was a shadowy Ch'u statesman-courtier of the fourth–third century B.C. He was politically active during one of the most crucial periods in Ch'u history, when the southern state fought several feudal wars and then followed with negotiations. Allegedly a man of great loyalty and social conscience, Ch'ü Yüan pleaded time and again with the reigning Ch'u prince on behalf of the war party (and, therefore, the long-range welfare of the people), but the prince was not responsive. Legend has it that after many a heart-rending protest, Ch'ü resorted to death by drowning as a gesture of despair. The germ of the legend is contained in the *Ch'u tz'u*, a collection of mournfully lyrical poems supposedly written by Ch'ü Yüan himself. For more details of the Ch'ü Yüan biography, see Hawkes, *op. cit.*, pp. 11–15.

33. See James J. Y. Liu, *The Chinese Knight-Errant* (London: Routledge & K. Paul, 1967), pp. 3, 68–70, 196–97.

34. See J. D. Frodsham, *The Poems of Li Ho* (Oxford: Clarendon Press, 1970), p. xvii ff.

35. *Ibid.*, pp. xxviii, xlix, lvii; Chou Ch'eng-chen, *Li Ho lun* (Hong Kong, 1971), pp. 159–64. There are several interesting points of resemblance between Kung Tzu-chen and Li Ho: (1) both wrote two antipodal kinds of verse—biting social satires and introspective poems with strong Buddhist overtones; (2) both used archaic language in satirical verses—Li's "Ballad of the Savage Tiger" (Frodsham, p. 189) strongly recalls Kung's "Ease of Travel" (K 440) (It is likely that Han Yü influenced both Li and Kung, for they all had a predilection for archaic words.); and (3) both were attracted by the *Ch'u tz'u* language and its unique imagery. However, it should be pointed out that Li Ho's language is much more sensuous than Kung's; Li Ho's evocative use of color to symbolize emotion is in particular an "aberration" as well as a unique contribution to Chinese poetry.

36. Frodsham, *op. cit.*, p. xxx. This line suggests a similar sentiment expressed in Kung's "Petty merits, ornate writings,/ How could they be the aim of my life!" (K 564) and "Even though my writings may startle the empire,/ They contain nothing but living beings on paper." (K 565)

37. For T'ao Ch'ien's sword imagery and his ambivalent feeling about social responsibility and posthumous fame, see Hightower, *op. cit.*, pp. 137–38, 140–41, 143–44, 147, 171–72, 182, 224–25.

38. See Ramon Woon and Irving Lo, "Poets and Poetry of China's Last Empire," *Literature East and West,* IX (1965), 4:331–61.

39. "My hand writes what my mouth says" translates *wo-shou hsieh wu-k'ou* (from Huang's *Tsa kan,* or "Miscellaneous Thoughts," in Ch'ien O-sun, ed., *Jen-ching-lu shih-ts'ao chien-chu, chüan* 1). This remark of Huang Tsun-hsien's is neither daring nor new. Chin Sheng-t'an (1610?–61) and Yüan Mei had expressed similar views before, although in a more sophisticated way. See James Liu, *The Art of Chinese Poetry,* pp. 73–76; John Wang, *Chin Sheng-t'an* (New York: Twayne Publishers, 1972), pp.

39–43. Kung Tzu-chen also observed in one of his poems: "The elegant and the vernacular came from the same source . . ./ The beauty of a literary piece lies in its naturalness" (K 487). Perhaps because of similar views on poetic language and because of Kung's strong interest in the introspective self, some critics have associated him with Yüan Mei's *hsing-ling* or "native sensibility" School. See Chu Chieh-ch'in, *op. cit.*, p. 97; Tanaka, *op. cit.*, Preface, p. 9; and and Su Hsüeh-lin, *op. cit.*, (article), p. 740. For Huang Tsun-hsien's role in the renovation and liberation of classical Chinese poetry, see *Chung-kuo chin-tai wen-hsüeh-shih kao* (Shanghai, 1960), pp. 119–64; Ch'en Shou-yi, *Chinese Literature: A Historical Introduction* (New York: The Ronald Press, 1961), pp. 625–28; Julia Lin, *Modern Chinese Poetry: An Introduction* (Seattle: University of Washington Press, 1972), pp. 20–27.

40. Kurata, *op. cit.*, pp. 256 and 528.

41. For the development of modern (vernacular) Chinese poetry, its Western inspiration, and its organic relationship with the indigenous folk-song tradition, see Hsu Kai-yu, *Twentieth Century Chinese Poetry: An Anthology* (New York: Doubleday & Co., 1964), pp. xi–xxxix.

42. Wu Mi is among those who think Kung was a major influence on Huang. Wu cites Huang's medleys "Evening by the Lake of Compassion" (*Pu-jen-ch'ih wan-yu shih*), "Miscellaneous Thoughts at Sea" (*Hai-hsing tsa-kan*), and "Miscellaneous Poems of the Year Chi-hai" (*Chi-hai tsa-shih;* same title as Kung's, but much less in number) as evidence of Kung's influence. All these are seven-character *chüeh-chü*. See Wu Mi, *K'ung-hsien shih-hua*, in *Wu Mi shih-chi* (Shanghai, 1935), p. 155. Ch'en Yen, in his *Shih-i-shih shih-hua* (Taipei, 1961; *chüan* 3, p. 2b), also attests to Huang's fondness for Kung's poetry; and Ch'ien Chung-shu (*op. cit.*, p. 29) has specified that Huang's seven-character quatrains resemble Kung's.

43. Shao Tsu-p'ing, "Ch'i-yen chüeh-chü t'ung-lun," *Hsüeh-shu shih-chieh*, I (1936), 8:88.

44. See Kurata, *op. cit.*, pp. 249–56, 502.

45. Wu Mi, *Yü-sheng sui-pi, op. cit.*, p. 26.

46. Nan-she, or Southern Society, a name deliberately chosen in defiance of *Pei-t'ing*, or Northern Court (i.e., the Ch'ing Court), was an association of "revolutionary" writers formed in 1909. The society was supposedly the "largest association of Chinese writers of all times" and had, at its peak, a membership of over one thousand. See Liu Wu-chi, *Su Man-shu* (New York: Twayne Publishers, 1972), pp. 68–72.

47. The political reformers' basic tenets in the "new" poetry were emotional sincerity and social relevance. See *Chung-kuo chin-tai wen-hsüeh-shih kao*, pp. 119–31; Julia Lin, *op. cit.*, pp. 18–20.

48. Ch'ien Chung-shu, *op. cit.*, p. 161; Su Hsüeh-lin, *op. cit.* (article), p. 743; Kurata, *op. cit.*, pp. 250–52; and *Chung-kuo chin-tai wen-hsüeh-shih kao*, p. 149.

49. Liu Ya-tzu (1887–1958), founder of the Southern Society, considered Kung Tzu-chen his favorite Ch'ing poet. See Liu Wu-chi, *op. cit.*, p. 70; Kurata, *op. cit.*, pp. 502–4.

50. Kurata, *op. cit.*, p. 520.

51. For examples of Yang Ch'üan's "assembled verses" (*chi chü*) which are composed of lines by Kung Tzu-chen, see Wu P'u-an, ed., *Nan-she ts'ung-hsüan* (Taipei, 1966), III: 1214.

52. Ts'ao Chü-jen, *Lu Hsün nien-p'u* (Hong Kong, 1970), p. 130. Hsü Shou-ch'ang (1882–1948), a fellow native villager and good friend of long standing of Lu Hsün, is the source of this observation.

Selected Bibliography

Since all the books and articles referred to in this study have been cited in full in the footnote section, the following bibliography includes only those items which either are directly related to Kung Tzu-chen or have a special bearing on Ch'ing poetry.

1. The edition of Kung's collected works used in this book.
Kung Tz-chen ch'üan-chi. Ed. Wang P'ei-cheng. Shanghai: Chung-hua, 1959. 2 vols., has a 12-page introduction and a supplement containing Wu Ch'ang-shou's chronological biography of Kung, prefaces to various editions of Kung's collected writings, and a list of Kung's missing works. The poems are given in chronological order, with notes on variant wordings in other editions and brief identifications of the people mentioned by Kung.

2. Other editions consulted.
Kung Ting-an ch'üan-chi. Shanghai: Kuo-hsüeh fu-lun she, 1915. 7 vols.
Kung Ting-an ch'üan-chi. Taipei: Shih-chieh, 1960.
Ting-an ch'üan-chi. Pao-chen-chai edition, 1898.
Ting-an ch'üan-chi. Shanghai: Sui-han-chai edition, 1932.
Ting-an ch'üan-chi. Ssu-pu pei-yao, vols. 2269–72.

3. Annotated selections of Kung's poems.
Chin-tai shih-hsüan (Anthology of Modern [Chinese] Poetry). Peking, 1963. Begins with Kung Tzu-chen and concludes with members of the Southern Society, including Liu Ya-tzu and Su Man-shu. Kung is represented by a selection of 27 of his *shih* poems in different verse forms.

TANAKA KENJI. *Kyo Ji-chin* (Kung Tzu-chen). *Chūgoku shijin senshū* (Chinese Poets Series), ser. 2, vol. XIV. Tokyo, 1962. Contains a 31-page introduction to Kung's life and works, including his poetry; 163 pages of word-by-word commentaries on 83 of Kung's *shih* poems; and a chronological chart.

4. Chronological biographies *(nien-p'u)* of Kung.

HUANG SHOU-HENG. *Ting-an nien-p'u kao-pen.* In the Sui-han-chai ed. of *Ting-an ch'üan-chi* (see above). Most entries are very brief.

WANG SHOU-NAN. *Kung Tzu-chen hsien-sheng nien-p'u.* In *Ta-lu tsa-chih*, XVIII (1959), 7:11–15, 8:24–30, 9:20–29. Includes information culled from Kung's writings which the other two *nien-p'u* do not have.

WU CH'ANG-SHOU. *Ting-an hsien-sheng nien-p'u.* 1900. Comprehensive and easily accessible; appended in many editions of Kung's collected works.

5. Translations.

KOTEWALL, ROBERT, and SMITH, NORMAN. "Miscellaneous poems of the year Chi-hai, V," *The Penguin Book of Chinese Verse* (Penguin Books: Baltimore, 1962), p. 71.

LI , TERESA. "A Parting Song" (Miscellaneous Poems of the Year Chi-hai, No. 5), *T'ien Hsia Monthly*, IX:3 (October, 1939): 328.

YANG HSIEN-YI and YANG, GLADYS. "Kung Tzu-chen: Poems," *Chinese Literature*, 1966, No. 4, pp. 89–93. Translation of six *shih* poems; four, including No. 5, are from the Chi-hai medley.

6. Miscellaneous studies on Kung.

CHANG TSU-LIEN. *Ting-an hsien-sheng nien-p'u wai-chi* (Records in Addition to the Chronological Biography of Mr. Ting-an). In *Chüan-ching-lou ts'ung-k'o*, vol. IV, Shanghai, 1921.

CHANG YIN-LIN. "Kung Tzu-chen 'Han-ch'ao ju-sheng-hsing' pen-shih k'ao" (An Examination of the Facts behind Kung Tzu-chen's "Song of a Scholar of the Han Dynasty"), *Yen-ching hsüeh-pao*, XIII (1933): 203–8.

————. "Yü Ch'en Yin-k'o lun ju-sheng-hsing shu" (A Letter Discussing the "[Han-ch'ao] ju-sheng hsing" with Ch'en Yin-k'o), *Yen-ching hsüeh-pao*, XV (1934): 254.

CH'EN HENG-TE. "Ts'ung Lu Hsün t'an-tao Kung Ting-an" (Talking from Lu Hsün to Kung ting-an), *Ku chin*, No. 40 (1943). Reprinted in *Ta hua*, No. 41 (January, 1968), pp. 14–17.

CH'EN KENG-P'ING. "Shih lun Kung Tzu-chen" (An Attempt at a Discussion of Kung Tzu-chen), *Kuang-ming jih-pao wen-hsüeh i-ch'an*, Nos. 277 and 278, September 6 and 13, 1959.

CH'IEN MU. "Kung Ting-an ssu-hsiang chih fen-hsi" (An Analysis of the Thought of Kung Ting-an), *Kuo-hsüeh chi-k'an*, V (1935), 3:151–82. Same as the chapter on Kung's thought in Ch'ien's *Chung-kuo chin san-pai-nien hsüeh-shu shih* (Chinese Intellectual History during the Last Three Hundred Years); Taipei, 1957.

CHOU SHAO. "T'an Kung Ting-an" (A Talk on Kung Ting-an), *Jen-chien-shih*, XXXV (1935): 13–15.

CHOU TS'E-TSUNG. "Kung Ting-an te shih ho tz'u" (Kung Ting-an's *Shih*

Poetry and *Tz'u* Poetry), *Kuo-kuang tsa-chih*, XVIII (1936): 6. I was not able to obtain this article.

CHU CHIEH-CH'IN. *Kung Ting-an yen-chiu* (Studies on Kung Ting-an). Taipei, 1966. (First published in Shanghai, 1940; another Taipei reprint, in 2 vols., in 1965.) The chapter on Kung's poetry originally appeared in *Kuang-chou hsüeh-pao*, I (1937), 2:1–32.

CHU PO-SUNG. "Kung Tzu-chen so-hao te hsi-fang chih shu shih shen-mo shu" (What were the Western Books that Kung Tzu-chen liked?), *Kuang-ming jih-pao*, July 15, 1964.

FANG TZU-CH'UAN. "Hsing-ling tz'u-jen Kung Tzu-chen" (Kung Tzu-chen, the *Tz'u* Poet of Native Sensibility), *Fu-tan hsüeh-pao*, III (1936): 4. I was not able to obtain this article.

FU-TAN TA-HSÜEH CHUNG-WEN-HSI. *Chung-kuo chin-tai wen-hsüeh-shih kao* (History of Modern Chinese Literature, a Draft). Shanghai, 1960. Pp. 15–38 on Kung, including a 11-page discussion of his poetry.

HOU WAI-LU. *Chin-tai chung-kuo ssu-hsiang hsüeh-shuo shih* (History of Modern Chinese Intellectual Thought). Shanghai, 1947. Pp. 609–42 on Kung as pioneer intellectual and political theorist.

HSIAO I-SHAN. *Ch'ing-tai t'ung-shih* (A Comprehensive History of the Ch'ing Period). Taipei, 1963. Pp. 1764–92 on Kung's life and works, with emphasis on his political thought.

HUMMEL, A. W. *Eminent Chinese of the Ch'ing Period*. Washington, 1943–44.

KANDA KIICHIRO. "Kyo Tei-an no 'Ch'iu-yeh t'ing Yü Ch'iu-p'u t'an p'i-p'a' no shi ni tsuite" (Concerning Kung Ting-an's poem "Listening to the Lute Music of Yü Ch'iu-p'u on an Autumn Night"), *Ishida hakushi shōju kinen tōyōshi ronsō* (1964; commemorating the birthday of Dr. Ishida), pp. 195–203.

KURATA SADAYOSHI. "Shin matsu min sho no shidan ni oyoboshita Kyo Tei-an no eikyō" (The Influence of Kung Ting-an on Poetry Circles in Late Ch'ing and Early Republic Times), *Kagawa daigaku gakugeibu kenkyū hōkoku*, I:12 (August, 1959): 116–48.

————. (Shin matsu min sho o chūshin toshita) *Chugoku kindai shi no kenkyu* (Study of Modern Chinese Poetry, focusing on Late Ch'ing and Early Republic Times). Tokyo, 1969. Incorporates the article above in one of its chapters.

MEI YING-CH'AO. "Ya-p'ien chan-cheng shih-ch'i te chin-pu shih-jen Kung Tzu-chen" (Kung Tzu-chen, the Progressive Poet of the Era of the Opium War), *Kuang-ming jih-pao wen-hsüeh i-ch'an*, No. 161, July 16, 1957.

MENG SEN. "Ting-hsiang hua" (Lilacs), in *Hsin-shih ts'ung-k'an*, III: 39a–50a. Shanghai, 1936.

SU HSÜEH-LIN. "Ch'ing-tai nan-nü liang ta tz'u-jen lien-shih te yen-chiu" (Studies on the Love Affairs of Two Great *Tz'u* Authors of the Ch'ing Period), pt. II. *Wen-che chi-k'an* (Wu-han University), I (1937), 4:

737–42. This article can also be found in *Wen-hsing ts'ung-k'an* (Taipei, 1967), No. 235, with a biography of K'u-t'ai-ch'ing appended.

TAI HUNG-SEN. "Tsen-yang chieh-shih Kung Tzu-chen te liang-shou shih" (How to Interpret Two of Kung Tzu-chen's Poems), *Kuang-ming jih-pao wen-hsüeh i-ch'an*, No. 469, July 12, 1964.

WEI CHI-TZU. "Yü-ling shan-min i-shih" (Anecdotes of the Mountain Dweller of Yü-ling), in *Ku-hsüeh hui-k'an*, No. 13.

WENDHUT, ANNEROSE. *Kung Tzu-chen: Leben und Werk.* Dissertation, University of Hamburg, 1953; n.p. 79 pages of text proper, footnotes included.

7. Selected references related to Ch'ing poetry.

AOKI MASARU. (Shindai bungaku hyōron shi) *Ch'ing-tai wen-hsüeh p'ing-lun shih.* Tr. Ch'en Shu-nü. Taipei, 1969.

BIRCH, CYRIL, ed. *Anthology of Chinese Literature*, vol. II. New York, 1972.

CHANG TSUNG-HSIANG. *Ch'ing-tai wen-hsüeh.* Hong Kong, 1964 (reprint).

CHAO I. *Ou-pei shih-hua.* Shanghai, 1917.

CH'EN NAI-CH'IEN, ed. *Ch'ing ming-chia tz'u.* Hong Kong, 1963.

CH'EN YEN. *Shih-i-shih shih-hua.* Taipei, 1961 (reprint).

CHENG CH'IEN. *Hsü tz'u-hsüan.* Taipei, 1955.

CHIANG JUN-HSÜN. *Tz'u hsüeh p'ing-lun-shih kao.* Hong Kong, 1966.

CH'IEN CHI-PO. *Hsien-tai Chung-kuo wen-hsüeh shih.* Hong Kong, 1965 (reprint).

CH'IEN CHUNG-SHU. *T'an-i lu.* Hong Kong, 1965 (reprint).

CH'IEN O-SUN. "Che-p'ai shih-lun," *Hsüeh-shu shih-chieh*, I (1935), 4:17–29, 5:61–76.

———. *Jen-ching-lu shih-ts'ao chien-chu.* Hong Kong, 1963.

HO KUANG-CHUNG. *Lun Ch'ing-tz'u.* Singapore, 1958.

HSÜ K'O. *Ch'ing-tai tz'u-hsüeh kai-lun.* Shanghai, 1926.

HU YÜN-I, ed. *Ch'ing-tai tz'u hsüan*, in *Tz'u-hsüeh hsiao ts'ung-shu.* Hong Kong reprint, n.d.

KURATA SADAYOSHI. (Shin matsu min sho o chūshin toshita) *Chugoku kindai shi no kenkyu.* Tokyo, 1969.

LIANG CH'I-CH'AO. *Yin-ping-shih shih-hua.* Appended in *Liang Jen-kung shih-kao shou-chi.* Taipei, 1967.

LING SHAN-CH'ING, ed. *P'ing-chu Ch'ing-shih tu-pen.* Shanghai, 1932.

LIU, JAMES JO-YÜ. "Ch'ing-tai shih-shuo lun-yao," in *Hsiang-kang Ta-hsüeh wu-shih chou-nien chi-nien lun-wen-chi*, I (1964): 321–42.

LIU WU-CHI. *Su Man-shu.* New York, 1972.

LIU YA-TZU. *Nan-she chi-lüeh.* Shanghai, 1940.

LUNG YÜ-SHENG (Mu-hsün). *Chin san-pai-nien ming-chia tz'u-hsüan.* Shanghai, 1956.

———. "Lun Ch'ang-chou tz'u-p'ai," in *T'ung-sheng yüeh-k'an*, I:10 (September 1941): 1–20.

NIEN SHU. "Shih-t'an Chou Chi Chieh-ts'un-chai lun-tz'u tsa-chu," *Wen-hsüeh i-ch'an tseng-k'an*, IX (1962): 96–110.

T'ANG KUEI-CHANG, ed. *Tz'u-hua ts'ung-pien*. Taipei, 1967.

WALEY, ARTHUR. *Yuan Mei: Eighteenth-Century Chinese Poet*. New York, 1956.

WANG CHUNG, ed. *Ch'ing-tz'u chin-ch'üan*. Taipei, 1965.

WANG FU-CHIH, et al. *Ch'ing shih-hua*. Shanghai, 1963.

WOON, RAMON, and LO, IRVING. "Poets and Poetry of China's Last Dynasty," *Literature East and West*, IX (1965), 4:331–61.

WU HUNG-I. *Ch'ang-chou p'ai tz'u-hsüeh yen-chiu*. Taipei, 1970.

WU MI. *Wu Mi shih-chi*. Shanghai, 1935.

WU P'U-AN, ed. *Nan-she ts'ung-hsüan*. Taipei, 1966.

WU TUN-SHENG, ed. *Ch'ing-shih hsüan*. Taipei, 1967.

Index

(The works of Kung are listed under his name)